RICHMOND *Handbooks* FOR TEACHERS

Series Editor : Paul Seligson

An Introduction to *Teaching English to Children*

Susan House

Richmond
PUBLISHING

Richmond Publishing
19 Berghem Mews
Blythe Road
London W14 0HN

ISBN: 978-84-294-5068-2
Depòsito legal: M-26267-2008
Printed in Spain by Palgraphic, S.A.

Design   Jonathan Barnard
Layout   Gecko Limited
Cover Design   Geoff Sida, Ship Design

Illustrations   Steve Lach, Gecko Limited, John Plumb & Liz Roberts

Author's Acknowledgement
Thank you to Inés Alpuente and all the staff at the CRA de Villanueva de Alcoron, Guadalajara, for their help with the problem of mixed-aged groups in rural schools.

Map of the book

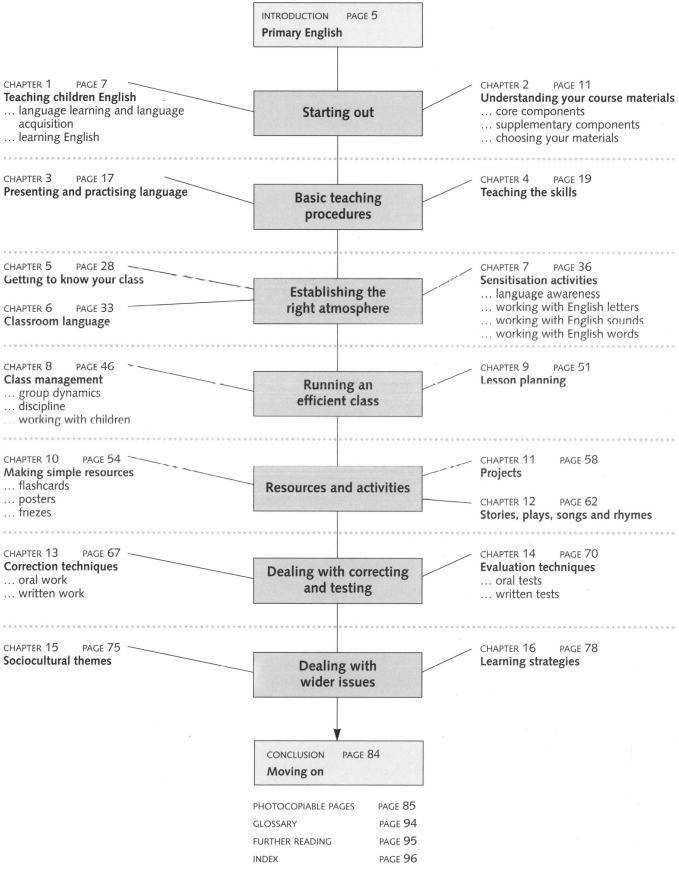

Richmond Handbooks for Teachers: An introduction

This series presents key issues in English Language Teaching today, to help you keep in touch with topics raised in recent educational reforms. The books all contain a mixture of analysis, development work, ideas and photocopiable resources for the classroom. The key note throughout is what is **practical**, **realistic** and **easy to implement**. Our aim is to provide a useful resource which will help you to develop your own teaching and to enjoy it more.

While each of the books has been written for the practising English Language Teacher in the primary or secondary environment, they are also suitable for teachers of languages other than English, as well as for teachers of young adults, trainee teachers and trainers.

All classroom activities are designed for lower-level classes (from beginners to lower intermediate) as these form the majority of classes in both primary and secondary. Most of them can, however, be easily adapted to higher levels.

The books all contain:

- *a section of photocopiable activities and templates.* These are either for immediate classroom use (some with a little adaptation to suit your classes) or for use throughout the year, e.g. assessment record sheets or project work planners.

- *regular development tasks.* These ask you to reflect on your teaching in the light of what you have just read, and some ask you to try new ideas in the class. They are all intended to make the ideas in the books more accessible to you as a classroom teacher.

- *an index of activities.* As most teachers dip into or skim through resource books, there is an index at the back of each book to help you find the sections or ideas that you wish to read about.

- *a comprehensive glossary.* As one of the main principles of the books is ease of use, the authors have tried not to use jargon or difficult terminology. Where this has been unavoidable, the word/term is in SMALL CAPITALS and is explained in the glossary at the back. Likewise, we have avoided abbreviations in these books; the only one used which is not in current everyday English is L1, i.e. the students' mother tongue.

Although all of the ideas in these books are presented in English, you may need to explain or even try some of them, at least initially, in the students' L1. There is nothing wrong with this: L1 can be a useful, efficient resource, especially for explaining methodology. New ideas, which may challenge the traditional methods of teaching and learning, can be very threatening to both teachers and students. So, especially with lower-level classes, you can make them less threatening by translating them. This is not wasting time in the English class, as these ideas will help the students to learn/study more efficiently and learn more English in the long term.

Primary English

"Who is this book for?"

This book has been designed to help teachers who may be embarking on teaching primary English for the first time. It will be useful for teachers who:

… already teach English but are about to teach children for the first time

… already teach children but are about to teach English for the first time

… are training to teach English to children.

The prospect of choosing your course materials, preparing your teaching programme, delivering your classes, evaluating your students and dealing with day-to-day problems in the classroom may seem initially daunting. You will find guidance and suggestions in this book that will make your teaching year not only easier to manage but more enjoyable for both you and your students.

If you have experience in teaching English to adolescents and adults, this will be invaluable for understanding the language itself. However, you will find that the characteristics of the primary student are very different and you will need to alter your approach considerably. You will need to adapt your expectations both with respect to your students' progress and your classroom management.

The primary school programme can cover many age ranges depending on the specific policy of your education authority or the school you are working in. Teachers working in this field often find themselves seriously challenged by the enormous range of basic abilities in their classrooms (reading and writing, dexterity and motor ability), not to mention other problems such as mixed-age classes in rural areas. We shall look at some of these problems and see how developing your own skills will help you to deal with specific issues relevant to the primary school environment.

You will find that different chapters in this book deal with these problems and offer you ways of coping with them in the classroom. The book starts with general issues and progresses to the more specific, and goes from the beginning of the school year to the end, but it is written in such a way that you can dip into chapters as the need arises. You will find references throughout the book to guide you to the issues you are interested in.

"What happens at the beginning of the school year?"

At the beginning of your course it is likely that you will be presented with a series of course materials for your classes. Or, if you are lucky enough, you may be asked to choose them for yourself. This book will attempt to show you how you can choose those materials and use them to your greatest advantage. We shall also look at introducing your own materials without having to increase your workload substantially.

Different publishers use different terms to describe the various components of a language course and the activities within those components. Do not be put off by this. They all follow the same basic pattern, which is described in Chapter 2.

"How do I use this book?"

You can use the Contents page to guide you through your year's work and the issues dealt with in this book. Likewise, it can help you locate topics you are interested in. The index (page 96) can help you find particular activities and topics as well.

"What will I need in the classroom?"

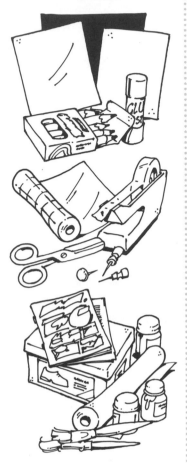

The following is a 'shopping list' of the items that you will need to do the activities described in this book and in many courses for younger children.

Everyday items

You will find these items useful for many activities in the primary classroom.

Glue: the stick kind is the cleanest to use in the classroom.

Coloured pencils: your students should have their own but you will need a supply for the classroom.

Card: in as many different colours as possible. Black is good for mounting wall charts.

Scissors: several pairs of round-ended safety scissors.

Drawing pins: the ones with coloured heads are easier to find if they fall on the floor. (These should be kept out of children's reach.)

Sticky tape: several rolls.

Transparent adhesive plastic covering: expensive, but useful for keeping things in good condition throughout the year.

Shoe boxes with lids (any size): ask the students to bring these in. They are useful for activities and for storing materials.

Paints and paint brushes: simple poster paints are the best.

White paper: the kind used as lining paper for wardrobes. This is for friezes and projects.

Magazines, comics and newspapers: ask the students to bring in old printed material.

Special items

These are useful for specific activities in this book.

Safety pins: these are useful for some activities and are always handy if the students are acting. (They should be kept out of children's reach.)

A washing line: long enough to be hung across the classroom.

A sheet or large piece of material: together with the washing line this can be used for activities and is useful for providing a 'stage' for acting activities, either as the curtain or the backdrop. You can glue or pin scenery onto it.

Clothes pegs: four or five.

Bathroom scales

Measuring tapes or long rulers

Some of these objects can be provided by the children themselves while others may be provided by the school.

TIP

Keep all of these things in a box in the staff room if you do not have an 'English classroom'. Make sure that you keep any potentially dangerous objects out of the children's reach.

Which items in the second list above have you used with children? How did/would you use them? Check your ideas with activities 2–4 on pages 28–31 of this book.

CHAPTER 1

Teaching children English

Language learning and language acquisition

We distinguish the process that takes place when learning our first language (L1) from that of learning a second language by using different terminology. We say that the first language is **acquired** and the second language is **learned**. This is because we understand that the first language is acquired through experience while the second language usually comes with formal teaching. Language ACQUISITION takes place in a constantly stimulating environment: children are exposed to their first language from the very beginning and they are literally bombarded with language all the time. Although we cannot reproduce these circumstances exactly, we should try to provide our students with at least some of the stimuli which are present in language ACQUISITION in order to facilitate language learning.

If we think of teaching as the other side of learning, then by trying to understand better how children learn we will have more understanding of how to teach them. Learning is often confused with studying or memorising. Because we, as adults, have already acquired LEARNING STRATEGIES, we often confuse learning with studying. Studying is a tool for learning; it is not learning in itself.

Young children have hardly begun developing these strategies and are, therefore, at a more elementary stage of the learning process than an adult or adolescent. For young children, learning is still a question of experiencing rather than committing information to memory so we need to provide our students with the possibility of experiencing to ensure successful learning. Because children learn from experience, they do not distinguish learning situations from non-learning ones: all situations are learning situations for a child. This is an extremely influential factor for you to remember when you are working with primary school children because you will see that every moment of your time with your students is, potentially, learning time and you should take full advantage of this.

Let's look first at how we teach language and see how this affects the composition of a teaching unit.

The order of acquisition

Language is usually delivered in the classroom following an established belief regarding the order of language ACQUISITION: **listening, speaking, reading, then writing.** This means that we:

… present the language orally; the child **listens**
… then ask the children to reproduce this language orally; the child **speaks**
… then present language in the written form; the child **reads**
… finally ask them to reproduce this language in a written form; the child **writes**.

The four steps in this process follow this established order because it means that the child experiences language before reproducing it and that he/she experiences it in the oral form before the written form. By 'experiencing language' we do not mean that they simply hear or read something once and are then able to reproduce it perfectly; this does not happen even with the first language and it certainly will not happen with the second language.

Exposure to the language

It is important to take the matter of intensity of exposure into account when we assess our expectations of the children. Learning a language is above all a slow process. By the time the children come into the English class their first language is usually very developed. They have had eight or nine years of continuous exposure to this language; we are obviously not going to achieve the same results with a second language where their exposure over a year may be about eighty hours, if they are lucky!

Formal and informal practice

The four skills described above can be practised in the classroom both formally and informally. That is, the exercises in the course materials will provide formal practice but classroom communication also provides less formal practice, which is often integrated, of the four skills. You should take **maximum** advantage of this informal practice because it represents free communication.

The difficulties of reading and writing

With young learners we are essentially concentrating on listening and speaking. At primary level there are obvious constraints to the reading and writing skills. Some of your younger students may only just be managing to read in their L1 and others may not yet have fully developed the hand-eye co-ordination needed to write at any speed. In some cases, the children may not have fully developed their writing skills in their own language, and introducing them to writing in English could cause confusion, especially where similar words are concerned. Furthermore, different stages of development may be very marked, particularly at the beginning of the school year. You should not forget that, at this stage, the difference in development between a child who is eight years old in January and one who is not eight until December of the same year can be considerable.

Encouraging the learning process

You can use the following as guidelines for stimulating the learning process.

- Present language orally. The children need to listen to language on tapes as part of formal instruction and from you through informal communication in the classroom. Talk to the children in English and use natural language. ◆ SEE CHAPTER 6 Silence in the classroom should not be your aim. It is sometimes required for individual work but, if your classroom is silent most of the time, the children are certainly not listening to enough English.

- Spend a good part of your class time getting your students speaking. The purpose of language is communication. In the following chapters you will find several examples of activities designed to let the children use language.

- Your primary students need to read both from their course materials and informally in the classroom. There are many activities in this book which provide visual support for language, such as labelling the classroom and making posters. It is **extremely** important to let children play with letters and words as part of learning to read. If you are thinking about designing games and activities for reinforcing reading, always try to include a step which lets the children physically move letters around to form words. ◆ SEE CHAPTER 4

- Writing is the last skill that we develop in language learning. As can be seen from the four-stage process for language ACQUISITION, it is the most complex stage because it cannot be performed successfully until the other three stages are in place. One of the reasons why second language teaching is so often unsuccessful is that teachers spend too much time on writing activities.

Finally, remember that the children's L1 is their point of reference. Do not expect them to learn things in English which they have not already mastered in L1. If the children are not proficient readers in L1, they cannot be expected to read in English. If they cannot tell the time in L1, do not try teaching them this in English.

Learning English

We can now look at some of the peculiarities of the English language and how these factors can influence the way we teach English in the primary classroom.

English pronunciation

Ask anyone who has learned English as a foreign language what they find most frustrating about it and they will probably say that it is the pronunciation: the fact that the connection between the way words are written and the way they are pronounced is so apparently chaotic. Unlike many Latin-based languages, each letter in English does not have one independent, unchanging sound. Most vowels can be pronounced in two or more ways and, brought together in different combinations, they form different sounds. There are twenty different vowel sounds in English, all produced by just five letters (see page 60 for a list). There are many consonant combinations which produce different sounds, e.g. *th* can be /θ/ (as in *think*) or /ð/ (as in *this*). Additionally, there are some letter combinations which make certain letters silent, e.g. in words ending in -*e*, such as *take* and *hope*, the -*e* is silent; in the words *comb* and *lamb* the *b* is silent. These are just a few of the peculiarities of English sound-spelling correspondences. As if this were not enough of a problem, English, unlike many languages, does not use accents to show where a word should be stressed. You have to know where to put the stress.

You may find a selection of exercises in your coursebook which are designed to help the children to deal with this issue. But remember: correct pronunciation is only developed by **listening** to English and reproducing the sounds. Reading English will not help with pronunciation.

English structure

At primary level we are usually concerned with simple structures, such as basic verb tenses, adjective/noun combinations, prepositions and so on. The structural objectives for the whole first year of English should be very limited and should be practised and recycled continually.

Structure should not be taught independently from the whole language context. If, for example, you are concentrating on the possessive 's, start by showing the children how the structure works: take an object from a student's desk and say, e.g. *Look! This is Miguel's pen and this is Paula's book.* With children it is much better to demonstrate the language than to explain it.

Language learners need to **use** structures. This means that they have to be practised in the classroom both formally, using the course materials, and through classroom communication. It is best to limit your course objectives to a few structures and to work again and again with these same structures, using different vocabulary and putting them in different situations.

You should distinguish clearly between the structures that you expect the children to be able to produce and those that you expect them only to understand. When we tell a story in the classroom, the text of the story may contain complex structures, but the children can follow the story from the non-linguistic support such as pictures, sound effects and gestures. We cannot expect the children to produce these structures for some time.

However, our ultimate aim in the classroom is to teach our students effective communication. This means that they should be able to understand and make themselves understood in an ever-increasing number of situations. An efficient communicator is not a person who knows a lot of structures, it is a person who knows how to use structures, quite often a limited number of structures, to communicate.

Motivation

An important element of successful teaching is knowing how to motivate your students. This is a complex issue since different people are motivated by different things. Motivation is not to be confused with competition. Competition is one of the strategies that you can use for motivation but it is by no means the only, nor indeed the best, strategy. Sadly, in many cases the only motivation provided in the classroom is that of passing exams!

The main motivation for language learning has to be the desire to communicate. Children want to communicate if they have something that they want to say to each other. We have to determine what language the children will want to use and how they will enjoy using it. This means designing the content and the methodology of our teaching accordingly.

Content

For young children the central interest is themselves. They love telling you and their peers about themselves, their possessions and their immediate surroundings. You can exploit this interest by PERSONALISING many of the activities that you do in class. ◆ SEE CHAPTER 3

As children get older their field of interest becomes wider and more varied. At the beginning of the school year you should spend some time getting to know what your students are interested in. When you are preparing your lessons, ask yourself if they will be interested in the activities that you are planning to do. See if you can alter the activity in any way in order to motivate their interest, e.g. football results and league tables are ideal for practising numbers and pop star posters are fun for using as illustrations for learning adjectives.

Methodology

Teaching a language is different from teaching other subjects in so far as our aim is communication. We cannot promote communication among the children if they are all sitting quietly doing individual work all the time. There is nothing motivating about learning a language if you are just going to do exercises in a book. By varying the GROUP DYNAMICS in the classroom we can provide the students with different types of interaction and a chance to develop the kind of social interaction that is necessary for any communication to take place on a regular basis. This, in itself, is an important motivating factor. ◆ SEE CHAPTER 8

You will also need to motivate children individually. Encouragement is by far the best tool for promoting and retaining a child's interest in English. You can encourage your students by making sure that your expectations are always within the individual child's abilities. Children are encouraged when they succeed but not when they fail. Failure and fear of failure sets up a harmful 'vicious circle', which often lasts for the student's entire schooling: the student fails once and perceives him/herself as a 'bad' learner. This in turn demotivates the student and makes him/her less likely to try because he/she believes that failure is inevitable. The need to encourage success is sometimes known as 'the feel good factor'. This has come under some criticism recently as a possible cause of lowering standards in schools. However, it doesn't mean that we should praise bad work, but that we should **avoid** it, by careful planning of each class to ensure positive motivation.

Look back at the headings in this chapter. Apply them to your primary class(es). Have you read anything here which you can do in your next lesson to help your students to learn?

CHAPTER 2

Understanding your course materials

The different components available in language courses vary from publisher to publisher. We can look at the components in terms of:

Core components	Supplementary components
Coursebook (Student's Book)	Flashcards (Activity Cards)
Activity Book (Workbook)	Posters
Teacher's Book (Teacher's Guide)	Student's Cassettes
Class Cassettes	Evaluation Pack (Test Book)
	Picture Dictionary
	Video Cassette
	Cut-out Book

Most publishers provide all the core components, but the supplementary components vary considerably. You can usually buy only the components you wish to suit your school and budget.

Core components

The coursebook

The coursebook is the main support for your classroom work. It will probably be in colour and is usually designed to be used as a reference book which should not be written in. Much of the work contained in this book will be for pairs and groups rather than for children working on their own. Coursebooks are usually divided into two types of unit and other materials.

Content units

These present new material and contain the basic syllabus of the book.

Revision units

These are designed to bring together the work you have covered over a number of units and to revise and sometimes extend this work into new contexts.

Reference material

At the back of the book you may find reference material such as lists of irregular verbs, word lists, extra activities, grammar summaries, and so on.

The activity book

The activity book is usually black and white and is designed to provide support and extension activities for the coursebook. The children are allowed to write, colour and often cut out in this book. Some of the work may be for groups but most of it will be for individual work. Since this book is designed for parallel use with the coursebook, the syllabus and the main features follow those of the coursebook, with the exception of the reference material. In this case you may find extension work on word lists or grammar summaries, or some seasonal activities such as cut-outs for Christmas cards or birthday invitations.

The teacher's book

This usually provides lesson plans for each class and some of them contain copies of the coursebook page and activity book page within the lesson plan. If your teacher's book does not contain these pages, you will need copies of the coursebook and activity book in order to plan your work.

The teacher's book may be in English or the L1. If the book is not in English, it should still contain language models in English for you to use in the classroom and model dialogues for student work. If you can choose either L1 or English for the teacher's book, choose the language **you** feel comfortable with. Do not feel obliged to use the English version if you think that it will create more work for you.

Syllabus information

The teacher's book should provide you with a syllabus (or map), usually at the beginning of the book, which will identify the objectives for your year's work. These objectives will be divided into language items, but may also have class procedures and activities for student development, e.g.

	End Activity	Drawings and Stories	Songs and Games	Language Target	
UNIT 1	The Classroom Game	Pupils draw and label the contents of their pencil cases.	The Colour Song 1￼ The Classroom Game	NEW￼ pen, pencil, book, rubber￼ Numbers 1-6￼ red, blue, green, yellow￼ yes, no￼ (Is it a) book?	
UNIT 2	Pupils fill in a wall planner with their birthdays.￼ Pupils make a birthday card for another pupil.	Pupils draw pictures to represent the months of the year.	The Months Song￼ Happy Birthday to You￼ Clock Bingo	NEW￼ Numbers 7-12,￼ My name's ...￼ How old are you? I'm ... (today).￼ Happy Birthday (to you)￼ Bingo￼ Love from	REVISION￼ Numbers 1-6￼ Yes, no￼ Red, blue, green, yellow￼ Pen, pencil, book, rubber

(From *Boomerang* 1 TB, Alison Blair and Jane Cadwallader, Richmond English 1994)

Reference information

You may also find some reference information at the beginning of the book, offering advice as to how to carry out the various activities such as games and songs, or how to exploit any special features of the course.

Lesson plans

The main section of the teacher's book provides you with detailed lesson plans. In some cases these will be step-by-step accounts suggesting how to exploit the activities in the class or they may be simply a list of activities in a suggested order.

Tapescripts

The tapescripts for the cassette work will also probably be somewhere in the teacher's book, either in each lesson plan as they come up or in a special section. If they are in a special section you may find it easier to mark the place using sticky notes, as in the illustration on the left.

Tests

Many teacher's books now contain short tests which you can use to assess your students' progress throughout the year.

Vocabulary lists

Finally, at the back of the book you will usually find a list of all the vocabulary in the coursebook and the activity book. This list may be divided into PRODUCTIVE and RECEPTIVE vocabulary.

Productive: the students are expected to produce these words.

Receptive: the students are expected to understand these words, not produce them.

T A S K

Look at the vocabulary list in your current course. Does it show PRODUCTIVE and RECEPTIVE words? If so, what is the proportion of PRODUCTIVE words to RECEPTIVE words? Do you agree with the words highlighted as PRODUCTIVE?

TIPS

The teacher's book is your main tool for use before, during and after the class.

- Check in advance for any extra materials you might need for an activity.
- You may need to ask children to bring something in for the next class, so always try to be at least one lesson ahead of yourself.
- Read the lesson notes and highlight anything you think is important as you are planning your lesson.
- Anticipate vocabulary problems. Think of synonyms or bring in pictures or objects to demonstrate words which are not illustrated.
- Plan your timing (SEE PAGE 51) and decide which activities you can omit if necessary. **Do not omit presentation activities.** Equally, do not always omit the same kind of activity (e.g. the pronunciation exercises) or you will signal to the students that this type of activity is not important.
- Think about recycling an activity from a previous lesson as an introduction to each class. Songs and rhymes are particularly suitable. (Many teacher's books suggest warm-up activities of this nature.)
- Find the correct tapescripts for listening activities.
- Check the balance between skills and GROUP DYNAMICS in the lesson (SEE PAGE 47). Forty-five minutes of writing on a Friday afternoon may seem tempting but it is asking for trouble!

Class cassettes

Listening exercises are an important element of language learning. Consequently all modern coursebooks have cassettes for classroom use. The coursework often includes several basic types of listening material.

Stories

Many primary courses exploit the use of story-telling in the classroom. These may be traditional stories, original stories written specially for the book, stories about the main characters in the book or factual stories. SEE PAGE 62

Songs and rhymes

In most courses you will find either a song or a rhyme, or even both elements, in each unit. The songs will be recorded on a cassette so you don't need to worry about not knowing the music! Some cassettes also contain 'sing along' versions for the songs with music only. SEE PAGE 65

Task listening exercises

These exercises involve the students listening to a text of some kind, then carrying out a task with the information they have heard, e.g. colouring in a picture according to instructions, writing numbers in a chart.

Pronunciation exercises

These are repetitive exercises designed to focus on pronunciation models. Different books will focus on different aspects of pronunciation, depending on the criteria of the author and market demands.

Modelling exercises

You may find model material on the cassette, e.g. models for games, situational dialogues and ROLEPLAYS. This can be used as a model for explaining an activity.

TIPS

- Find your place(s) on the cassette for the listening activities before the class. Write the counter numbers down if you have more than one activity.
- Check the volume from the back of the class.
- Direct the speaker(s) on the cassette recorder towards the class.
- Seat any children with hearing difficulties near the front of the class.
- Remember to set the counter to zero before you play a section so that you can rewind easily.

Supplementary components

Flashcards

These may be presented as illustrated cards or cards with words on, or they may be designed for the children to cut out, colour and write on. FLASHCARDS offer valuable classroom exploitation and if they are not available as part of your course materials, it would be worth making your own as part of the classroom work. SEE PAGE 54 FOR EXAMPLES

Posters

Some courses provide posters for classroom use. These may either illustrate the story or the main vocabulary sets for each unit. They are useful because they form a focal point for groupwork. As with FLASHCARDS, if your course does not have posters, it may be worth making your own.

Student's cassettes

One of the latest innovations in course publishing: children have cassettes of their own for self-study purposes. However, this is an expensive component and is not generally considered necessary for primary work. In some cases, children will be able to share cassettes if they live near each other, or you may suggest this component for children who are having difficulty keeping up.

Evaluation pack

Some publishers provide the teachers with a separate evaluation or test pack, with test sheets and marking schemes which you can photocopy (or the teacher's book may provide tests). If you do not have this component, you will have to write your own test papers. SEE CHAPTER 14

Picture dictionary

This is sometimes provided as supplementary material to a coursebook, or as part of the activity book. If not, it is not difficult to make your own picture dictionary as a class activity (there are suggestions in DEVELOPING RESOURCES FOR PRIMARY, in the same series). For older children, see suggestions for storing vocabulary on PAGE 80.

Video cassettes

Your choice of this component will depend on the facilities available in your school and the budget for the English department. There are both advantages and drawbacks to using videos in the primary school classroom.

Cover the chart below. Think of the advantages and disadvantages of using videos in the primary classroom. Compare your opinions with the chart.

Advantages	Disadvantages
Children respond well to visual aids. Most children are familiar with this medium. Children see active use of the language.	Children have a short concentration span. Extra organisation time in the classroom. Children are passive while watching.

In some cases, the publisher provides you with activity sheets to go with each episode on the video. If you do not have these, you will need to prepare some yourself.

TIPS

- Watch the episode you intend to use before the class.
- Find and read the script. Extract the key language from it.
- Check that your students are familiar with the key language; present some if necessary.
- Prepare a pre-watching activity to prepare the students for the language they will hear.
- Set the context for the programme. If you are using a story in episodes, you can do this by asking the students to tell you what happened in the previous episode.
- Prepare a worksheet, e.g. for younger children prepare an 'empty' comic page (i.e. frames only) to represent the different scenes in the story. The children draw the sequence of events. For older children and those with more language, add some key sentences from the script on the board and ask them to include these in their drawings.
- Only play short extracts. If you feel that an episode is too long for one session, find a suitable place to stop and use the second half in the next class.

Cut-out book

Some coursebooks have a cut-out or a sticker book (or section). Younger children love these books, but they are relatively unusual. There is no reason why you should not imitate this type of activity. Try making collages with pictures of key vocabulary or getting the children to cut out shapes or numbers and stick them into their books. If you prefer, this can be done as a group activity in the form of posters, e.g. if you have recently looked at a unit on animals, each group could make a collage of as many different types of one animal as they can find, e.g. dogs, cats, fish, birds.

Choosing your materials

In some cases, choosing materials may be your responsibility. Given the enormous variety available, you may well feel overwhelmed. However, if you bear in mind certain factors, you should be able to shortlist those materials which will most suit each class. It is then a question of personal preference.

The different books in a series are usually designed to be independent of each other but you must check what the children are expected to know **before** they start each coursebook. You may have to spend a little time at the beginning of the year bringing the children up to date. Also, some series use the same characters throughout. If you start with, e.g. Book 2 of a series, you will need to familiarise the children with the characters in the book before they start the course.

Guidelines for choosing materials

- Check new materials on the market.
- Check the core components and supplementary components provided.
- Check the price. Do not make children buy components that you are not really going to use.
- Check the balance between text and pictures. Do you think the children will like the characters and the illustrations?
- Check that the course will provide you with roughly the right number of teaching hours. Do not forget to include extra activities.
- Check the themes. Do you think that they are appropriate for the age group and the environment of your school (rural, urban, multi-ethnic, bilingual, etc.).
- Check the social attitudes displayed in the course materials. Look carefully at the illustrations: these are important for reinforcing social values.
- Check school records for the work the children did last year or ask their last teacher. The materials for their age group may be too easy or too difficult.
- Check the amount of recycling.
- Check the balance of the skills covered in the course materials. Older materials may have a heavy bias towards reading and writing activities which are not so suitable for modern primary school teaching methods.
- Check the overall presentation of the course materials. Do you find it easy to follow the sequence of activities?
- Check the style of the activities. Do you think that these will work for you?
- Check that the course materials provide you with all the features you would like to use, such as stories, songs and ROLEPLAYS.
- Check in the teacher's book for activities asking you to divide your class into several groups of four to five students. Can you use or adapt these activities?

PHOTOCOPIABLE PAGE 1 is designed for you to use as a checklist when you are shortlisting course materials.

T A S K

1 Look at the course materials you currently use. Do you make full use of all the components? Can you think of ways of making more use of them?

2 If you are currently thinking of changing your course, use PHOTOCOPIABLE PAGE 1 to analyse the suitability of alternative courses.

CHAPTER 3

Presenting and practising language

Most materials for teaching English, regardless of age group, offer a similar pattern for teaching new language in each unit.

Presentation

This is the first time that we introduce the children to the key language for the unit. Most coursebooks at primary level present new language through listening exercises, which are contextualised by the use of pictures or a story in the book.

If your book does not provide a cassette activity for language presentation, you should ideally do this yourself by giving the children a model of the word or language item. If you expect the children to say something they have never heard before, you may get some rather strange results due to the peculiar phonetics of the English language! For example, imagine asking a class of eight year olds to read the colours for the first time: *white, yellow, blue, purple* ...! The important thing with primary children is that language is presented in **context**; adults may be able to analyse language and refer to their L1 (often mistakenly!) to help them to understand, but children can't. They need a clear visual and/or aural context to understand.

Practice

Once your students have been presented with the new language, they practise it using the different skills of listening, speaking, reading and writing. If you look at activity headings or symbols in your coursebook, you will probably see the exploitation of the four skills. In most cases, the coursebook provides the oral activities and some reading tasks, while the activity book provides any writing tasks. The listening activities will be mainly in the coursebook. It is important that new language is practised first in a highly controlled way, e.g. the children recognise and produce the language in activities which have no ambiguity, such as a drill or responding to simple picture prompts. Once the children are more confident with the language, they can move on to freer activities where they have a choice in the language used.

Personalisation

This is a useful way to extend the free practice of a particular item in your teaching syllabus. PERSONALISATION consists of asking the children to apply the language structure they have just learned to themselves. In this way you show them that the language they have learned is useful to them and not just something written in a book. You reinforce the idea that language is a living, active and communicative tool.

For example, imagine you have just been looking at a unit on clothes. The following activities PERSONALISE the topic.

- The children tell you what they wear on different occasions, e.g. to visit their grandparents.
- They make a list of their favourite clothes and compare it with their friends.
- The children bring in their favourite clothes for the next class and have a fashion show. You can act as 'the commentator' and describe the children's clothes as they walk down the 'catwalk', which can simply be the aisle between their desks or across the front of the classroom. If your students' language skills are good enough they can then take over this role.

You may find some PERSONALISED activities in your activity book, in the shape of a picture frame where the children draw their favourite toy, clothes or pet. They may be in your coursebook in the form of guided dialogues where the children change key words. Or they may be questionnaire-type activities where the children have to ask the members of their group questions and compile a chart reflecting the opinion of the group.

These are easy alternatives to having the children moving around a lot, but it is fun to let them walk around the school asking other children about their preferences or for them to bring in their favourite toy or even pet!

If you wish to use PERSONALISATION activities which require slightly unorthodox practices, it is as well to check with the Director of Studies at your school whether or not these activities are permitted.

Recycling

As your students progress through the units they will accumulate more and more language. It is essential that they recycle this language very frequently so they do not forget the language they have learned in previous units. It is important not to rush children through the book at the expense of adequate recycling of previously presented language.

You will find several activities in each unit which recycle language from previous units. The amount of recycling needed increases as the children progress through the book. However, lack of space in coursebooks often means that language is not adequately recycled. If your course does not provide you with enough recycling, be sure to add activities yourself.

Think of language learning as a building task. Old language is incorporated into new structures. For example, the verb *have got* may be used again and again with different word families; the vocabulary set 'parts of the body' may be practised again using new adjectives or with the addition of the possessive adjectives.

Look at a unit from your coursebook which you have recently taught. Which of the activities are presentation, practice and recycling? Are any of them PERSONALISATION? If not, how would you plan a PERSONALISATION activity for this unit?

CHAPTER 4

Teaching the skills

 ## Listening

You can identify listening exercises by the title and/or a symbol of a cassette. But, remember, **you** are the best source of listening for your students. There are five basic types of listening tasks at primary level, as described below.

Stories

Many courses for children contain story work. Children respond very positively to story activities and these represent an important part of their language development. See CHAPTER 12 for ideas on how to use stories in the classroom.

Songs and rhymes

All coursebooks for young learners now contain a number of songs and rhymes.

In some cases these are traditional and in others they have been specially written for the book in order to reinforce vocabulary or grammar points. Both types have advantages and disadvantages.

	Advantages	Disadvantages
Traditional songs	usually well known; students may know the tune	often contain difficult and old-fashioned vocabulary
	important cultural input for students; often tell stories about life in English-speaking countries and can be extended into a sociocultural activity	perhaps more appropriate for native-teachers who know them from their own childhood
Specially-written songs	can be designed to practise a specific language point	do not form part of 'childhood culture'
	can use traditional music or music from songs in your own language, overcoming the problem of teaching the tune	if practising a specific language point, they can seem artificial and students may find them boring

Task listening exercises

These exercises will involve the students listening to a recorded text and performing some sort of task. The tasks may involve a physical response or filling in something in their activity books. They may be required to answer some questions about the text they have heard, usually orally.

Physical response activities

The theory of TOTAL PHYSICAL RESPONSE (TPR) suggests that children learn more easily if they react in a physical way to language stimuli. For example, the children hear a word and hold up a FLASHCARD which corresponds to the word or point to the corresponding picture in their coursebook, act out the word or hold up a smiley/sad face in order to register their feelings, and so on. You will probably find that there are several exercises like this, particularly in the coursebook.

Other task-based activities

In these activities the students are expected to do some sort of writing or drawing task, e.g. colouring in a picture, matching two columns or filling in the missing word.

In both cases it is important to remember that the object of the exercise is **understanding**. For this reason, you should play the tape several times. Here is an example of a dialogue and activities to accompany it. If you want to try some other activities, there is a students' answer sheet on PHOTOCOPIABLE PAGE 2.

Scene: A Sweet Shop

Characters: Bobby, Liz and Mrs Jackson, the shopkeeper.

SK: Hello, Bobby, Liz. Now, which sweets would you like today?
L: Hello, Mrs Jackson! Well, we need some sweets for Sam's party. Have you got any party bags?
SK: Party bags?
B: Yes, you know, the ones with a lot of different sweets.
SK: Oh, yes, I know what you mean. Now, let's see, I think there are some in here ... Here we are, how many do you want?
B: Oh. How many friends are coming to the party? There's Ellie, Sun Yi, Paul, Gabriella, Nitja.
L: With the three of us, that makes eight.
B: Oh! And Vanessa, Hammed and Boris. How many is that altogether?
SK: Eleven, so do you want eleven party bags?
L: Yes, that's fine, thanks. No, just a minute, twelve would be better, just in case. Yes, twelve party bags, please, Mrs Jackson.
SK: Here you are, dear, twelve party bags. Have a good party. 'Bye.
L & B: Thanks. 'Bye.

- Set the context, e.g. *This is a sweet shop*.
- Tell the students what their task is, e.g. *Listen. How many party bags do the children buy?*
- Play the tape through once and tell the children just to listen.
- Check understanding by asking a few general questions about the text, e.g. *How many children are in the shop?*
- Play the tape through again and tell the children to do the exercise(s).
- Play the tape a third time, stopping at convenient points and telling the children to check their answers individually or in pairs. This gives slower students an opportunity to catch up.
- If the exercise is a task activity, play the tape a fourth time while students correct their own or their partner's work. ◆ SEE CHAPTER 13

Pronunciation models

Many course materials now include short exercises on pronunciation and stress. Here, the emphasis is on sound, not meaning. We want the children to reproduce the sounds correctly. For this reason these exercises should be done without them looking at the words. The tapescript is usually a list of words with the same sounds or contrasting sounds. If your coursebook asks you to extend the exercise into a written contrast of sounds, e.g. the different vowel combinations which make up the same sound (*bear, hair, dare*), make sure that the students say the words out loud as they do the exercise. They will be tempted to change the pronunciation as they write the words and it is important that you correct them.

Modelling exercises

In some cases, activities which require students to perform guided dialogues or games involving student interaction in English will be modelled as an exercise on the tapes. You can use these exercises as preparation for the children to perform their own dialogues.

- Explain to the children what the activity entails.
- Play the tape and let them listen.
- There should be support for this material in the coursebook. Play the tape again and let the children look at the text in their coursebooks.
- For extra reinforcement, model the dialogue with a good student, or get students to explain the activity in L1.
- Ask them to perform the dialogue or play the game using their coursebooks as a guide at first.
- Tell them to continue but this time without reading from their coursebooks.
- Check pronunciation and play the tape again if necessary.

Speaking

Speaking exercises are identified by the title and often by a symbol representing the skill, e.g. a pair of lips or a speech bubble. Most teachers wonder how they can get their students talking more in class. First, we must remember that children at primary level are usually extremely limited in the amount of language they know. Free conversation is simply not possible, so all oral tasks have to take place in a very well defined framework, e.g. drills or simple ROLEPLAYS. SEE PAGE 23

Apart from the oral exercises that you do in class, remember that the children have the opportunity to speak English in their basic classroom communication and that this may be the only truly free communication that they will practise. For this reason, insist on their using English whenever they can (but don't expect them to perform beyond their abilities as this will only inhibit them).

Make sure that the students understand fully what they are expected to do. Many exercises fail to produce satisfactory results because they do not understand what is expected of them.

Oral drills

Oral drills are exercises which require students to listen to words, phrases or sentences and repeat them, sometimes changing a key item. They can become very monotonous and routine, especially if you have a large class and everybody has to have a turn. Here are some suggestions for livening up the drills.

Work in groups

If you have a large class, divide it up into smaller groups and let the group, rather than individuals, perform the drill. In this way you will not have all the other members of the class waiting for a long time until it is their turn.

Use stress, intonation and tone

Language can be altered by changing the **stress** and **tone**. The meaning of a sentence or phrase in English can be changed considerably by altering the **stress**. Explain to the children that by emphasising a particular word in the sentence or phrase, they can change the meaning of their words, e.g.

C1: *I **like** spaghetti.*
C2: ***I** like soup.*
C3: *I like **chocolate**.*

Explain to the children that by stressing one particular word you make it more important in the sentence. Similarly, let the children choose the **tone** of their sentence or phrase: draw these faces on the board for them to copy.

The students practise the drills in different ways.

- Each group chooses a face and performs the drill using the emotion suggested by the face. The other groups hold up the corresponding face.
- If the group chooses the angry face, the students can shout their sentence; if they choose the sad face, they whisper their sentence and so on.
- An extension to this exercise is to ask one group to choose a face and show it to another group, who says the sentence using the tone indicated by the face.

Use physical involvement

Always encourage the children to use non-linguistic elements when they are doing oral drills. It makes the sentence or phrase much more realistic and introduces the important element of TPR, e.g. in the *I like ...* drill described above, they could point to themselves when they stress *I*, rub their stomach when they stress *like* and lick their lips when they stress *chocolate*. In the drills where they change the tone, they could choose a suitable facial expression or hand gesture to reinforce the emotion.

Use language that students know

In language drills where students are expected to change one or two words and make up a series, e.g. they have the language structure *I like/don't like* and have to add appropriate nouns, make sure that the children understand fully what they are expected to put into the gap and have the language to do it. With younger children it is better to provide them with a limited field, e.g. tell them to use the food and drink that they have at dinner time. If you leave the field wide open, they may produce quite extraordinary sentences which, while grammatically correct, make no sense or do not fit the context.

True or false drills

If the language drill allows for it, let the children play *True or false*. This can be done where the drill requires the students to formulate statements, e.g.

C1:   *I like soup and bread.*
Class: *True?*
C1:   *No, false!*
C2:   *I like fish and chips.*
Class: *False?*
C2:   *Yes, false.*

This activity can also be performed in pairs.

Throw in wild cards

Once your students are more proficient, try throwing in 'wild cards' when they are doing a drill, i.e. give them a word which will force other changes, e.g.

T: *Soup and bread.*
C1: *I like soup and bread.*
T: *Fish and chips.*
C2: *I like fish and chips.*
T: *He.*
C3: *He likes fish and chips.*
T: *Doesn't.*
C4: *He doesn't like fish and chips.*
T: *Sandwiches.*
C5: *He doesn't like sandwiches.*
T: *They.*
C6: *They don't like sandwiches.*

Roleplays

These are small dialogues for practising a particular structure/function. You will probably have models for ROLEPLAYS in your coursebook. If not, you can easily make up your own by taking short dialogues out of the story. Some ROLEPLAYS are simple repetitions of dialogues and others require the students to replace key words.

The procedure for ROLEPLAYS is as follows.

- Students read and familiarise themselves with the (example) dialogue.
- Divide the class into pairs, A and B. Give A and B roles from the dialogue.
- Let students act out their ROLEPLAYS, not just say them. Students should read/prepare each line and then look up and say it, not just read it aloud.
- Walk around correcting and checking. ◆ SEE CHAPTER 13
- Students swap roles and repeat. Those who finish first can be asked to make up their own ROLEPLAY, using different words to fill the gaps.

ROLEPLAYING is the practice of situational speech. If you don't have any ROLEPLAYS in your coursebook, try thinking of typical situations for students of your age group, e.g. asking for information (the time, the date), asking permission to do something, inviting a friend, accepting an invitation, expressing surprise. Make sure that the language you use is natural spoken English.

Information gaps

Another type of oral activity in which students are asked to provide information that is missing or to correct information that is wrong. This is often done by contrasting what they hear or read with what they see, e.g. they see a picture of a garden and read or listen to a description of it. The description differs slightly from the picture, e.g. in the picture there are three people, but the description speaks of two. Students have to identify the differences or the missing people/objects. This activity is often done by the students first indicating the differences on paper by underlining or circling. They then say what the differences are, e.g.

T: *What about the people?*
C: *There are three people, not two.*
T: *And the time?*
C: *It's six o'clock, not eight o'clock.*

Acting

Many of the newer classroom materials now contain models for the students to act out scenes from stories. ◆ SEE PAGE 64

Reading

The number and extent of reading exercises that you do will be dictated by your students' reading skills. It is obviously not possible to demand reading skills in English if the children are not competent readers in their own language. A good rule for the teacher is: **Let the children read when they are ready to do so.**

The skill of reading

Reading involves two skills.

Decoding

This is the correct pronunciation and sounding out of the word and should always be done aloud and always following a model from the teacher or the tape when the language is first being presented.

Reading with understanding

This is when the student reads sentences or phrases and understands, preferably simultaneously. They will usually need to read the sentence or phrase more than once and should read in silence in order to concentrate on the meaning.

Don't worry if it takes some time before these two skills come together; with primary learners reading remains a two-stage process for some time. You should, therefore, adapt the reading activities to the age and skill of the students and this may well mean that some members of your class are ready to read before others.

As your students get older they will gradually be doing more reading exercises and more reading with understanding. However, as we saw earlier, at primary level the emphasis is on listening and speaking. It is advisable to treat all reading and writing exercises as listening and speaking exercises first, e.g. if the students have a reading comprehension exercise to do, read the text aloud or play the tape first while the students listen. Then ask one of the students to start reading aloud. (While reading aloud is frowned upon with older learners, it is useful with younger learners to help consolidate the sounds of the text.) Read the questions aloud while the students listen. They answer the questions, i.e. speak. The students can then perform the reading and writing exercise individually.

If you are working with pre-readers or rudimentary readers, try providing them with plenty of stimulus of **whole** words. Let them play with words as they are learning to read them. Labelling the classroom (SEE PAGE 42) is a good way to let them see words that they will be using frequently.

Another activity for this age group is decomposing and composing words.

ACTIVITY 1: LETTER JUMBLE

Level: beginners/elementary

Aim: word recognition

Group dynamics: small group/pairs

Language: classroom instructions: *write, cut and make words*; lexical set of your choice

Materials: strips of coloured card (as many colours as key words) 2cm wide and long enough to write words on

---

This exercise is to familiarise students with a word family or group of words that they have been working with, e.g. animals. It can be used with all words as long as the students have heard, said and seen the word previously.

● Divide the class into pairs or groups.

● Write the words you have chosen on the board.

● Give each group a set of cards and tell them to write each of the words onto a different coloured card, with each letter far enough apart so that they can then cut the word up into individual letters.

● The children cut up the words and then mix up all the cards.

● The group recomposes the words on the table, using English to say the letters where possible.

● Walk around checking the words and asking the children to read out the words.

Adapting for higher levels and older students

Try more sophisticated activities designed to develop reading with understanding, e.g. jumbling words and sentences rather than letters.

Guessing the meaning of unknown words

Children are sometimes put off reading because they are faced with words that they do not understand and assume, often wrongly so, that these words are obstacles to their overall understanding of the text. If your students are likely to be faced with examination work which requires them to do comprehension exercises, it is essential that you teach them how to deal with this problem.

● Choose a text from your coursebook.

● Tell the students to read it quietly and underline the words they do not understand.

● Tell them to read the text again and see how many of the words that they originally underlined they can now understand.

● Tell them to work with a partner and try to help each other to work out the meaning. They should look for clues to help them, e.g.

   1 If there is a picture, can they find a clue in it?
   2 Do they know if the word is a verb, a noun or an adjective?
   3 Does the word sound as if it should be something good or bad according to the context?
   4 Can they think of another word which would fit the context? Try it out. If it doesn't fit, try again.

Using readers

There is an enormous range of guided reading material on the market designed to encourage children to read in English. Using this material both encourages them to read and helps them to learn language outside the standard coursebook language and the classroom environment.

Choosing readers

● Choose books that will be interesting to your students, not necessarily books that you find interesting!

● Do not choose books that will be too difficult as they will discourage the students. It is a good idea to choose books that are slightly easier than you think they can cope with, at least at first.

● Not all students like the same kind of book. Be prepared to offer a variety to cope with different tastes.

- Choose books with pictures to help understanding. Children are encouraged by books that look attractive.
- Make sure that the first books you choose for children are short.
- Choose modern children's stories rather than classics because they are less culturally biased and the language is more appropriate.
- Some readers have accompanying cassettes. These can be very useful to encourage children who do not really like reading, but they do make the readers more expensive. It might be possible for the students to share cassettes.

▶ SEE FURTHER READING

Encouraging reading

It is surprising how many students are put off reading altogether or reading a particular author because of the way that this activity was dealt with in the classroom.

- Reading should be an enjoyable activity. Do not turn it into a task or exercise. Do not test your students on their readers.
- If you have the facilities, make a reading corner. This should be a quiet, comfortable place where the children can sit and read. You can partially section off this area with bookshelves and let them spend some time each week reading alone. This is particularly useful in mixed-ability or mixed-age groups.
- Do not set the pace for the children. Let them progress at their own pace.
- Monitor them in the following way.

  1 Ask the student if he/she is enjoying the book.
  2 Ask general information, e.g. *What is the name of the boy/girl in the story? Is it about England?*
  3 Ask the students to draw a picture about a particular event in their story or help them to tell you about it. Let them use a mixture of English and L1.
  4 When they have finished the book, ask them to write a book review. This should be very simple, e.g.

The title of my book is **An earful of aliens**
It is by Noel Ford.
My favourite character in the book is Professor Bucket.
I like this book because it is very funny.
This is my favourite part:

  5 The book reviews can be collected in a library file so that students can look at each other's reviews.
  6 Some readers have activities and exercises at the back of the book which can be done after each chapter or after reading the whole book. Look at the activities and choose the ones you think will be fun or let the students choose one or more. Do not make the students work through all the exercises.

Writing

The skill of writing

As mentioned earlier, your students' writing skills may well be at different stages of development. Writing consists of motor skills as well as language skills and younger children take longer to perform a simple writing task because their hand co-ordination is not fully developed. Written exercise types usually follow a set pattern of development to avoid this problem. Don't be tempted to rush the children through this development at too early a stage. Free writing is developed very slowly. **Do not expect students to write freely what they cannot say freely.**

Copying

Children copy words often by first tracing over a word in the activity book or writing it somewhere near the model they have to copy, in which case the whole word may be outlined for them or just the first letter to identify the word. Children need a lot of space to write in. When you are choosing your activity books for the younger age groups, make sure that there is enough space for writing. They also need a lot of time for writing, even copying.

Filling in

The children read a sentence/phrase which has a word missing and fill in the word by choosing from a list on the page, e.g.

> Choose from this list to complete the sentences: *one two three four*
> 1) People have _____ hands.　　2) I've got _____ head.
> 3) No animals have _____ eyes.　　4) Dogs have _____ legs.

Younger children may be given lines for each letter and/or the first letter; older children may have to provide the word from memory.

Altering/writing to a model

The students write a small passage changing key words to alter the meaning, e.g.

> Read this passage about Billy and then write about yourself.
> Billy lives in Manchester. He gets up every morning at half past seven to get ready to go to school. He usually has a big breakfast and then goes to school by bike.

Written comprehension

The students read a passage and answer questions. Initially they will be 'lifting' the answer from the passage and copying it as their answer. As the exercise becomes more sophisticated, they will have to use 'their own words'. At primary level this should mean no more than reorganising the words from the text.

Free writing

This is the ultimate objective in developing writing skills. All free writing must have a clear framework. You will be very disappointed with the results if you expect the children to produce a piece of written work entirely on their own initiative. Let them produce short pieces of work, making sure that you provide them with most of the vocabulary and all of the structure models they need.

Look at the practice exercises in two units of your course. Is each one focused on speaking, listening, reading or writing? Do any of them combine skills? How do they do this? Make a note of any techniques which are not described here.

CHAPTER 5

Getting to know your class

When you start the school year you may or may not know all the members of your class and, moreover, they may or may not know each other. During the course of the year they are going to work together in different group organisations and it is a good idea to try to set up a good working relationship among the members of the class at the beginning of the year. This means that they should all get to know as many of their classmates as possible, as should you.

Familiarisation activities

Here are some suggestions for activities which will help the class to work together. While the children are doing these activities, you will have the opportunity to learn their names and to observe the interaction taking place. You will be able to see who is assertive and active in group/pairwork and who is less able to assert themselves. This will help you when you have to divide the class up for group activities. The students will obviously speak L1 during these activities.

ACTIVITY 2: NAME BADGES

Level: beginners/elementary

Aim: student co-operation

Group dynamics: whole group

Language: classroom instructions, *My name is ..., I am* + age

Materials: one 10 × 5cm card per student, passport-sized photographs of students, glue, coloured pencils, one safety pin per student

---

Note: You will have to do this in your second or third lesson. Ask the children in the first lesson to bring in small photographs of themselves.

This activity is designed to encourage the students to organise themselves. Do not intervene in the organisation unless it is absolutely necessary. It is a valuable moment for you to observe the working dynamics of the class and to encourage social co-operation among the students.

- Ask the children either to glue a photograph of themselves onto the card or to draw a picture of themselves on it. Do one yourself to demonstrate. If some students have forgotten their photographs, let them draw themselves.
- They write their name and age on the card, e.g. *My name is Maria. I am eight.*
- When all the children have finished their badges, they pin them onto their chest. Ask them to organise themselves in a line in alphabetical order (using their first names). Do not be tempted to intervene at this point, although there will be a lot of L1 going on in the classroom. This is the moment when you can observe the interaction. Who is doing the organising, who is disagreeing and who is being organised?
- Check the alphabetical order and correct the line if necessary.

Other activities

You can perform different tasks using these badges, all based on the same principle of getting the students to organise themselves, e.g.

- The students organise themselves into two groups: names with six or fewer letters and names with more than six letters.
- The students organise themselves into two groups: names beginning with the first half of the alphabet (A–M) and names beginning with the last half (N–Z).

Adapting for older children

- Students could draw a picture of their favourite pop star or sportsman/woman and write, e.g. *I am Gloria Estefan.* Then proceed as before with the alphabetical organisation.

Adapting for higher levels: *Who am I?*

- Cut out pieces of card 5 × 2cm and write the names of famous people on them.
- As the children come into class, stick a card on each child's back with sticky tape. Don't let the child see the card on his/her back.
- The children have to ask each other questions to find out who they are. They can only answer with *yes* or *no*, e.g.

    A: *Am I a man?*
    B: *No.*
    A: *Am I from Europe?*
    B: *Yes.*

- They continue until they guess the name stuck to their back. Do not limit the students to one partner only. Let them walk around asking several students. Choose funny characters but be careful not to make any one student the centre of fun. Until you know your students well, it is wise not to make them too self-conscious.

After you have observed the students organising themselves, make a note of what you think might be good working groups. Try these out in the classroom. Did they work as you expected? If not make adjustments.

ACTIVITY 3: WHOSE FEET?

Level: beginners/elementary

Aim: getting to know the class

Group dynamics: whole group

Language: classroom instructions, *This is* + name

Materials: a length of washing line (long enough to be hung up across the room), a sheet, four or five pegs

---

This is a fun activity in which the teacher has to identify the children by looking only at their feet! Done at the beginning of the school year, it is a wonderful ice-breaker and shows the students that English classes are going to be fun. It also helps you to learn their names!

- Hang a washing line across the classroom at about 1.7m above the floor.
- Hang a dark sheet up across the washing line with pegs, so that the bottom of the sheet is about 25cm from the floor.
- Tell the children to stand behind the sheet so that you can only see their feet and part of their legs. If you are feeling adventurous, you can ask them to take off their shoes and socks so you can see their bare feet. If the class is very

29

big, the children will have to do this in small groups. The others can watch and laugh!

- Try to identify the children just by looking at their feet. Use natural language that you feel comfortable with. They may only understand their names but they will hear you speaking in English, e.g.

T: *Let's see. This is Maria.*
Class: *No!*
T: *Well, Roberto, then.*
Class: *Yes.*

- As you identify the children, they stand in front of the sheet, until all the class has been identified.

- Alternatively, you could do the same activity using the children's hands. In this case, hang the sheet so that the bottom is about one metre from the floor.

ACTIVITY 4: INFORMATION CHARTS

Level: beginners/elementary

Aim: getting to know the class

Group dynamics: small groups/pairwork

Language: classroom instructions, various

Materials: card, coloured pencils, bathroom scales, measuring tape

---

There are several charts that you can make at the beginning of the school year to provide you with useful information throughout the rest of the year. Remember to vary the type of chart. The activities described below are good for cross-curricular work because they fit in particularly well with maths activities. You could check with the maths teachers about the type of charts the students are working with and use the same type. The charts should be mounted and pinned up on the wall (if possible) for later use when the students are practising specific language structures. If you can't put them on the wall, keep them safely in the staff room so that you can bring them to class when necessary.

Choose the type of chart which best illustrates the information. In each case below, one type is suggested but you can use other types.

Birthday wheel

Language: *Whose birthday is it this week/month? Which is the most/least popular month for birthdays?*

All children like to be the centre of attention on their birthday. You can make a point of playing popular games when it is somebody's birthday and singing *Happy Birthday To You*. Make a birthday wheel at the beginning of the year and ask students to check whose birthdays take place each week/month.

Preferences pie charts

Language: *Twenty-five per cent of our class likes beans.*

This type of diagram is for showing proportions and will work well with questionnaire-type activities. If you have questionnaires or surveys in your coursebook, you can get the students to transform this information into pie diagrams. Check with the maths teacher for cross-curricular activities.

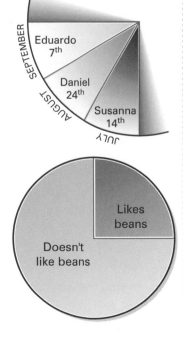

Height and weight line graphs

Language: *Now I am one metre 44cm. I weigh 40 kilos.*
I have grown two cm this term. I have put on three kilos.
Who is the tallest/the shortest/the heaviest/the lightest in the class?
Maria is taller/heavier than David.

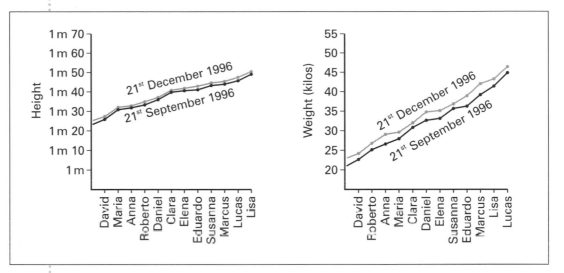

Children like to monitor their growth. Make the diagram at the beginning of the year and chart their growth at the beginning and end of each term.

Note: Be sensitive to variations in your class. Don't insist on weight charts if you have any heavy children in your class.

Changes in nature flow chart

Language: conjunctions: *and then, after that, before that, so, finally*

At primary school students are working a lot with changes in both themselves and the world around them. Flow charts are effective ways of illustrating this process of change. With older students you could use these charts to display learning strategies.

Family tree

Language: *This is my mother.*
I've got three brothers.
My father's name is Daniel.

a seed

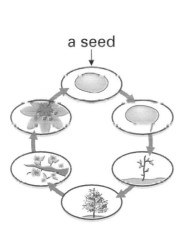

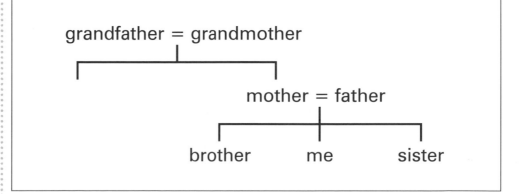

Choose the complexity of the family tree according to the age group of your class. Younger children should deal only with the immediate family (grandparents, parents, brothers and sisters), but older students can work with a complex family.

Note: When dealing with families most of us come up against the situation of a student who has no mother or father, or one who has step-parents. You cannot avoid this issue; just deal with it naturally. You may need to reassure the student in L1 at this point. Depending on the social environment of your school you may need to introduce other family words. It is important to reinforce the idea that there is not only one type of acceptable family group, but many varieties.

Rules for the classroom

At the beginning of the school year you can establish the working rules for activities in your class. You will probably have to remind students of the rules throughout the year, especially before a potentially noisy activity! PHOTOCOPIABLE PAGE 3 is an example of a 'charter' (contract) which you can photocopy, enlarge and pin on the wall. You will have to explain the rules in L1 at the beginning of the year, but the illustrations next to each rule will reinforce the idea.

If you anticipate particular discipline problems, try this approach.

- Divide the class into teams at the beginning of the term.
- Give each team a name, e.g. a colour or an animal.
- Make a chart for the wall and give each team 100 points to start the term.
- Explain that every time one member of a team breaks the rules, his/her team will lose a point.
- Count up the points at the end of the term and award a prize to the team with most points.

It is important that you group the students in such a way that a 'difficult' student is placed in a group with 'co-operative' students. If you put all the 'difficult' students in the same team, you will need more than 100 points! Alternatively, you could try using forfeits. SEE PAGE 66

If, by the end of the first term, you are still having problems of student integration and some students always seem to be left out of groupwork, get the students to make a Christmas card and tell them that it is for their 'invisible' friend. Inside the card they write *Happy Christmas to my friend, from David*. Let them decorate the card as they wish. On the last day of term put names into pairs carefully, making sure that you bring together students who are not working well together, and give each student the name of his/her invisible friend on a slip of paper. Before the students leave for the Christmas holidays, they exchange their Christmas cards.

Think about any specific behavioural problems you are experiencing in class. Can you think of a way to negotiate with the student(s) in question? How could you make them feel responsible for a particular task in class, something to co-operate with the running of the class?

CHAPTER 6

Classroom language

It is important to remember that, for many students, their only contact with the English language will be through their teacher. If you feel comfortable using English freely in the classroom, do so. Use natural language, speaking clearly and not too fast and pay particular attention to your intonation and gestures. The students will often capture the overall meaning of what you are saying by identifying non-linguistic features. Imagine, for example, that you can't find a book. Say to the students *Oh dear, now where is that book? I've looked on the shelf, in my bag ... I can't find it anywhere!* They will understand the word *book*, especially if you repeat it, and they will guess from your gestures and intonation that you are frustrated and you are looking for a book. If you point to the shelf and your bag as you say the words, they may also pick up on these, so be as visual as you can. This is a **vital** step in communication and will encourage them to listen for things that they **can** understand.

Using L1 in the class

We often wonder about the amount of communicating we should do in L1 in the classroom. Not long ago, teachers were urged never to use L1 in the classroom. Thankfully, most of us now realise that this is simply not practical. There are times and situations where L1 is the fastest, most efficient and most appropriate form of communication with our students. However, you should always use English in the classroom where this **is** a feasible vehicle for communication. Present your classes in English as far as possible, reinforce communication in English between the children by providing them with the language that they need for this communication and insisting on their using English when working together whenever they can.

There are times when it is useful to use L1.

- Sometimes it is necessary to spend a little time speaking in L1 in order to introduce a particular theme, especially sociocultural themes. ◆ SEE CHAPTER 15

- You will almost certainly need to use L1 for serious disciplining. If students are not used to hearing you speaking too much L1 in the classroom, when you do want to get serious it can have quite an effect!

- As a general rule, you should try to use English to explain an activity to the class, but sometimes L1 may be necessary. If so, first think about whether this activity is really appropriate for the children's ability. You could always give the instructions in English first and then in L1.

- You may find it useful to use a mixture of the two languages with older/higher-level students to help them through explanations of difficult structures, but do not encourage them to translate structures into or from their L1. Show them that they can translate nouns (not including abstract nouns and proper nouns) by looking up words in dictionaries or thinking about how they would say them in L1, but do not encourage translation of full sentences or other language parts, e.g. prepositions, as this could confuse students.

Try to get used to speaking in English in the classroom even when you know the students will not be able to understand you completely, pause at key words and point or use gestures to give them the opportunity to follow what you are saying. When you first start the school year, try to always use exactly the same expression for routine actions, e.g. as you start the class say *Hello, everyone, take your books out.* Once the students are familiar with one form of introduction, vary it so that they don't get too dependent on one expression. There is a notorious example of one little boy who, when he was asked how he was, always answered with *I'm fine, thank you, and you, Miss Rosalind?*

The students will gradually build up classroom language. It is important to insist on students using language which they have learned in class. A good rule to establish in the classroom is **Always use English when you can.** Initially this will produce a sort of hybrid language, but they will gradually move towards more and more English.

For the general day-to-day running of the class, the students should be introduced to essential classroom language as soon as possible.

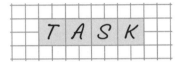

Look at your lesson for the next class in your teacher's book. Can you think of how to 'explain' the activities to your students without using L1? What body language can you use to help?

Essential classroom English

We can divide this into two basic categories.

Teacher language

This is language you use that your students need to understand and which forms the basis for classroom instructions that will be used throughout the year. See PHOTOCOPIABLE PAGE 4 for some of the common teacher instructions. You can enlarge this to make a wall poster and point to the instructions as you say them until the students are familiar with them. Make your own wall chart for other instructions if you wish.

Student language

Apart from the teacher's instruction language, the students should gradually incorporate expressions of co-operation for pair/group interaction and student-teacher communication. It is in this area that you have to be particularly insistent that they should always use English whenever they can.

Here are some examples.

Teacher language	Student language
Sit down.	*Hello.*
Stand up.	*Goodbye.*
Open your (course)books.	*Yes.*
Look.	*No.*
Listen.	*Please.*
Colour the ...	*Thank you.*
Write.	*Can I borrow your pen?*
Cut the ... out.	*Can I go to the toilet, please?*
Touch the ...	*I'm sorry!*
Don't do that!	*That's (not) mine.*
That's good/fine/nice.	*My turn!*
Be quiet.	*Me!* (very useful for games)
Show me.	*Here you are.*
Tell me.	*That's right.*

Obviously, you cannot introduce the teacher instructions all together. Try introducing them in pairs, e.g. *Sit down/Stand up*. When the children have heard and responded to or acted out these instructions a few times, play a *Simon Says* game (in some course materials this is called *O'Grady says*). *Simon Says* is an easy game both to teach instructions and to get the children to burn up a bit of energy.

- To start with, you take the role of Simon. You say, e.g. *Simon says 'Stand up!'*
- The students say *Stand up* as they do the action.
- Teach students **not** to do the action if you **don't** say Simon says, i.e. if you just say *Stand up*. Any student who does the action in this case is 'out'.
- Increase the number of different instructions as the students learn them. The students mime the instructions or perform the actions.
- Once the students have played this game several times you can let them take turns in giving the instructions to the rest of the class. This can also be played in pairs or small groups of four or five.

Try also using small ROLEPLAYS for some student language, e.g.

- Divide the class into pairs.
- Tell each student to take four things out of his/her pencil case and place them on the table in front of him/her.
- The students practise asking each other if they can borrow things, e.g.

  A: *Can I borrow your pencil, please?*
  B: *Yes, here you are.*
  A: *Thank you.*

Give the students two or three expressions each week and ask them to learn them. You can set a date for everybody to learn all the expressions, giving them enough time to do so. Tell the students that after this date you will subtract team points (SEE PAGE 32) or make them perform a forfeit if they use L1 for any of these expressions. Always give them the opportunity to repeat something in English, because sometimes they may be so absorbed in their activity that they simply forget to use English!

T A S K	Think about your classes. Can you think of any other examples of language that *you* often use, or that your students use which you can translate into English and use in English from now on? Think particularly about the language that students use when they are working in English.

CHAPTER 7

Sensitisation activities

At the beginning of the school year, while you are trying to get to know your class and they are getting to know you, you will find it useful to do some sensitisation activities. These prepare your students for learning another language. You will probably find it necessary to use L1 during these activities.

Language awareness

Sensitisation to language can work on two levels.

Awareness of other languages in general

If you are lucky enough to have students in your class whose L1 is different from their classmates', or who are perhaps bilingual, take advantage of this.

- If you have several other language speakers in your class, divide the class up into groups with one 'other language speaker' in each group. If not, work as a whole group.
- Set the group(s) the task of learning something simple in the other language, e.g. *My name is David, I'm ten years old*. The other language speaker(s) acts as the teacher. You may find this very useful for integrating students from other ethnic groups.
- When each group has learned its 'new language', children can practise their sentences in class.

If you do not have other languages in your class, work as a whole group and try to think of words that you use in your own language which are from other languages. Technology is a good field for this activity.

- Ask the students to name all the words from other languages that they can think of and to say where these languages are spoken.
- Ask them if they know how to say anything in any of these languages. Prompt them when you can.

Awareness of the English language

A successful sensitivisation exercise is to prove to the students that they actually already know quite a lot of English. We are fortunate that the language we are teaching is English, as the use of English is so widespread that practically all our students, no matter how young, will already know a few words in English, although they may not be aware of this. Most children know the following words and expressions:

… *OK*
… the numbers *1, 2, 3*
… the instructions on a computer
… expressions from football: *penalty, corner, goal*, etc.
… words from pop songs or at least the name of the album/compact disc (in the case of older students)
… slogans on T-shirts
… commercial brand names of sweets, soft drinks and other consumer items.

Try setting up a competition between groups of four or five children to collect as many English words and expressions as they can in the first week. They can exchange new words and expressions at the end of the week. The group with the most is the winner. Let them explain where they found or heard the word/ expression and what it means. This activity will, hopefully, persuade the students that they already know some English and that it is not so difficult.

Working with English letters

Teaching the alphabet

Teaching the English alphabet is surprisingly difficult because the names of the letters do not correspond to the sounds of the letters in speech. However, it is generally one of the first exercises in all coursebooks because it is useful for spelling and listening exercises. Here are some activities to help your students to work with the letters in English.

ACTIVITY 5: THE ALPHABET PYRAMID

Level: beginners

Aim: to distinguish the different sounds of letters in English

Group dynamics: whole group/pairwork/individual

Language: classroom instructions, the alphabet

Materials: one 12 × 12cm card per student

This pyramid shows the letters of the alphabet in 'sound' groups:

/iː/	B C D E G P T V
/e/	F L M N S X Z
/eɪ/	A H J K
/uː/	Q U W
/aɪ/	I Y
/əʊ/	O
/ɑː/	R

- Draw the pyramid on the blackboard.
- Practice the sounds with the class several times.
- The students copy the alphabet pyramid onto their cards.
- Clean the blackboard. Write a letter on the board and point to a student and ask him/her to say the letter.
- At first students can use their pyramid as a reference. Gradually ask them to identify the sound without referring to the pyramid.

Other activities

- Draw the pyramid on the blackboard and rub out some of the letters. Write the letters you have erased around the pyramid. Ask the class to place them correctly in the pyramid.
- Draw the pyramid with some of the letters wrongly placed. Ask the class to identify them and place them correctly.
- Students colour their pyramid with different colours for each line and practise in pairs, spelling their names and those of their families or friends.

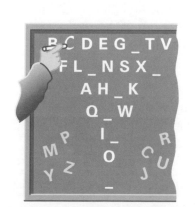

ACTIVITY 6: SECRET CODES

Level: beginners

Aim: to familiarise students with the letters and letter combinations

Group dynamics: whole group/pairwork

Language: the alphabet, numbers 1–26, classroom instructions

Materials: one 12 × 8cm card per student

- Write the alphabet on the board with numbers underneath each letter.

  A B C D E F G H I J K L M N O P Q R S T U V W X Y Z
  1 2 3 4 5 6 7 8 9 10 11 12 13 14 15 16 17 18 19 20 21 22 23 24 25 26

- Tell the students to write their names on card in the number code with a slash (/) between each number. Write your name on the board as an example, e.g. 19/21/19/1/14 (Susan).
- Collect all the cards and give one to each student at random.
- The students work out whose name card they have and stand up when they know whose it is.
- Ask the students who are standing up to spell out the name on the card.

Other activities

- Make different codes, e.g.

    … number the letters from 26–1

    … use shapes and colours instead of numbers (A = red triangle, B = blue circle, C = yellow square and so on)

- Write the names of objects in code. Students work out the name and touch the object or say the name of the object.
- Write commands and ask the students to carry them out, e.g. choose one of the codes and write three instructions on the board in code, such as *Stand up, Open your book, Sit down.*
- Students work in pairs, sending messages to each other in code.

ACTIVITY 7: MAKE A BOOKMARK

Level: beginners

Aim: to make a personalised item using letters of the alphabet

Group dynamics: individual

Language: the alphabet, classroom instructions

Materials: one 5 × 15cm card per student, scissors, glue

- Students draw and cut out the first letter of their first name and glue it on the top of their card, so that it can be seen slightly above the top of the card.
- They write their name vertically down the bookmark in felt-tip pen or coloured pencil.

Other activities

- Students can draw objects on the book mark beginning with the first letter of their name. This can now be used to keep their place in the coursebook.

```
pen  book
school bag
sharpener
ruler  rubber
```
```
book
pen
rubber
ruler
school bag
sharpener
```

M	E	Y
L	S	T
P	D	J

Listening for letters and numbers

ACTIVITY 8: LETTER CLASSIFYING

Level: beginners

Aim: to classify words in alphabetical order

Group dynamics: whole group

Language: the alphabet, classroom instructions, vocabulary set of your choice

---

For this activity make sure that your students are familiar with the task of putting words in alphabetical order in their own language.

- Write a series of words on the board from the most recent vocabulary set the students have been studying, making sure that no two words begin with the same letter.
- Ask the students to write or call the words out in alphabetical order.

Other activities

- To complicate the activity, add words beginning with the same letter so that students have to look to the second or third letter.
- Ask them to classify the words according to whether they begin with a vowel or a consonant.
- Students can choose a word (or you can give them the word) and then form a line in alphabetical order according to their word. Students with the same word stand together holding hands.

You could also use more traditional language games for letter and number work, such as Bingo. Bingo is probably the most popular and the most versatile game of all. You can literally play bingo with everything! The following is a game of bingo described for the alphabet, but you can equally use numbers, words or phrases.

- Each student makes a bingo card with nine 'boxes' either on a piece of card or in their exercise books.
- Tell the students to fill in the squares with one letter in each square.
- Call out the letters at random, while the students cross off the letters on their card as you call them out. Make sure that you keep a note of the letters you have called out, so that you can check the 'winner's' card.
- The first student to cross out all the letters calls out *Bingo!* You check that he/she has heard all the letters correctly. If so, he/she is the winner.

Note: This game can be played as a whole group, in small groups or in pairs.

You can perform many simple listening exercises using letters and numbers.

ACTIVITY 9: FAMOUS TELEPHONE NUMBERS

Level: beginners

Aim: to practise recognition of letters and numbers

Group dynamics: whole group

Language: the alphabet, numbers 1–10, classroom instructions

- Make up a list of about ten famous hero figures for your students (pop stars, historical figures, television characters, sportsmen and women) and their 'telephone numbers'.

- Tell the students to listen to the list of the famous people and then choose five people they would like to telephone.
- Read the list of famous people again, but this time read their telephone number as well, e.g. *Gary Barlow's phone number is 381 9763.*
- The students listen and write down the numbers of the people they have chosen.
- Read the list again so that they can check.
- You can then write the full list on the board for students to check their phone numbers.

Note: Make sure that you tell the students that these are not really the famous people's telephone numbers or you may find that their parents have an extraordinary phone bill at the end of the month!

A variation on this activity is car registrations. These are useful for working with letters, numbers and countries. You can use either national car registrations or international registrations and ask the students to identify the country as well.

- Read out five car registrations, e.g. B 2784 HL, M 8395 CB.
- Students write down the registrations.
- Read the list again for the students to check.
- Write the registrations on the board or ask students to write them on the board.

Working with English sounds

Overcoming the pronunciation problems of English

Teaching sounds at primary level is important for future pronunciation, especially once the students begin to read English. Focus on the vowel sounds first, as these are the most difficult.

ACTIVITY 10: SOUND MATCHING

Level: beginners

Aim: to distinguish specific vowel sounds

Group dynamics: small group/pairwork

Language: classroom instructions, phonemic distinctions of your choice

Materials: one copy of PHOTOCOPIABLE PAGE 5 for each student

- Make enough copies of PHOTOCOPIABLE PAGE 5 to go round the class. Cut off the last four words, which are wild cards and do not have the same sounds as the rest. Keep these for more complicated versions of the activity. Give each student a copy and tell them to cut along the dotted lines until they have all the words on separate pieces of paper.
- Check that they know the two sounds /u:/ and /ɒ/; practise them with one or two familiar words first.
- Hold up one of the cards and say the word, stressing the vowel sound. The students find this word and place it face up on the table.
- Now tell students to find all the other words on their cards that have the same sound. They put them all in one pile.
- Students can now play in small groups or pairs. Walk round checking the sounds.

Other activities

- Complicate the game by throwing in one or some of the wild cards (the last four cards on the page).
- Play the game as a memory game. Place cards face down on the table. Students have to find matching vowels by turning over the cards and trying to remember where the correct words are.

Now do this activity with other sounds that your students have problems with, e.g. /b/ and /v/ or /æ/ and /ɑː/. Think of simple English words containing these sounds, prepare them and do the activity.

ACTIVITY 11: RHYMING WORDS

Level: beginners

Aim: to recognise rhyming pairs

Group dynamics: whole group

Language: classroom instructions, individual words of your choice

---

- Write about ten words on the board at random, making sure that you have five rhyming pairs, e.g. blue/shoe.
- Check that the students can reproduce each of the words with the correct pronunciation.
- Ask students to put the words into five rhyming pairs.

Adapting for higher levels

- Write five words with different sounds on the board and ask students to think of rhyming words.
- Write the rhyming words on the board as above but add a couple of words that do not rhyme with anything. Tell students that there are some words that don't rhyme and ask them to identify the words.

As you are working with different sounds you might like to make a Sound Book over the year.

- Use a large scrapbook with different coloured pages or make your own with coloured paper and card for the cover.
- Assign one double page per sound. Use the first single page as an index.
- Let students take it in turns in pairs to be responsible for a page in the book.
- As you finish working with a particular sound, either stick pictures of the words in the book or write the words themselves in it (or do both).
- When new words arise during the year, you can ask students to look for the right page in the Sound Book to put in the new word, or if necessary to make a new page.
- You can choose the number of pages you wish to work with according to the age of the students. Younger students can work with the long and short vowels only (12). The older students could work with all twenty vowel sounds.

Working with English words

Helping students to remember vocabulary

Many teachers worry that their students do not retain the vocabulary that they learn in the course of a school year. Of course, they will not remember absolutely everything, but you can help them to 'store' their words in ways which will help them remember. Classification activities are good as memory exercises. Quantity is not important: your students don't need to know all the names of animals in English, for example, but they should be able to remember a few from each type, i.e. farm, wild and domestic. Playing with words is an important feature of all language learning. It helps students to overcome the mystery of the foreign language and is invaluable for memory retention. Here are some simple activities which you can use as individual exercises, pairwork or team games.

> **ACTIVITY 12: LABELLING THE CLASSROOM**
>
> **Level:** beginners/elementary
>
> **Aim:** word/object correspondence
>
> **Group dynamics:** whole group
>
> **Language:** classroom instructions, classroom vocabulary
>
> **Materials:** 12 × 8cm cards, drawing pins and sticky tape

- Decide on a list of useful classroom objects, e.g. *window, door, board, table, chair, book, pencil, rubber, ruler, scissors.*
- Write the words on the cards and pin or stick the cards on the objects.
- Students can draw the smaller objects on a large card and make a poster for the wall.
- Encourage the students to use these words in English, even if they do so in the middle of a sentence in their own language.

Other activities

- Tell the students to close their eyes while you change the labels around. The students must then put the labels back in the correct place.
- Turn the labels so that the words are facing the walls and the students cannot see them. Ask them to try to remember as many of the words as possible.

If your classes are not always in the same room, keep your labels in a box and make one student (a different one each time) responsible for bringing the labels to the classroom and putting them up.

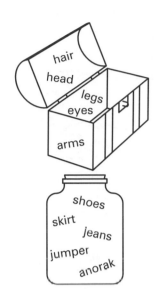

ACTIVITY 13: CLASSIFYING WORDS

Level: beginners/elementary

Aim: to classify words into logical groups

Group dynamics: pairwork/individual

Language: classroom instructions, key vocabulary of your choice

Materials: PHOTOCOPIABLE PAGE 6

- Choose two of the 'containers' on PHOTOCOPIABLE PAGE 6, enlarge if possible and make copies for each student.
- Choose the type of classification you want to use. These can be lexical sets, structures (e.g. all past tense together), word functions (e.g. nouns, verbs), etc.
- Present the words to be classified. You can do this in a number of ways: on the board, using FLASHCARDS or by asking the students to find them in Letter Boxes. ◆ SEE PAGE 60
- Tell the students to write the words in the different containers, e.g. one type of word in one container, another in the second container.

ACTIVITY 14: HIDDEN WORDS

Level: beginners/elementary

Aim: decomposing and composing words

Group dynamics: pairwork/individual

Language: classroom instructions, key vocabulary of your choice

- Identify the key words you want to practise, e.g. parts of the body.
- Make a grid (as below), divide each word in two and write each half in one of the boxes at random.
- Students find the words and recompose them.

HE	SE	EY	MOU	LE	AR
TH	GS	AD	NO	MS	ES

Key: head, nose, arms, eyes, mouth, nose

- The game becomes more complicated as you add more boxes and words. Longer words may be split up into three or more boxes.

ACTIVITY 15: DOMINOES

Level: beginners/elementary

Aim: decomposing and composing words.

Group dynamics: pairwork/small groups

Language: classroom instructions, key vocabulary of your choice

Materials: 5 × 10cm cards

Dominoes is a very versatile game which can be used to help word recognition and spelling.

- Choose key words and split the words between two dominoes, as below.
- Students play dominoes: each student has a number of dominoes. In pairs/ small groups, they create words by putting the correct dominoes side by side.

Other activities

- Give the students another word family and ask them to make another set of dominoes in pairs or small groups.

ACTIVITY 16: ANAGRAMS

Level: beginners/elementary

Aim: word recognition, composing and decomposing words

Group dynamics: pair work/individual

Language: classroom instructions, key vocabulary of your choice

Materials: strips of cards 3cm wide

Anagrams are words where the letters have been rearranged. They are traditionally solved by writing out the letters in different formations until the correct word is found, but with children it is easier and more fun if they can physically move the letters around to find the solution.

- Choose key words and mix the letters up in each word to form an anagram.
- Write the anagrams on the board, with the real words at random around them.
- The students write the first anagram on the card in large letters, and cut it up into letters. They then move the letters around until they have a word.
- Continue until all the anagrams have been solved. The students can then invent anagrams for their partners.

ACTIVITY 17: CARD GAMES

Level: beginners/elementary

Aim: word recognition, saying words

Group dynamics: pairwork/small groups

Language: classroom instructions, key vocabulary of your choice

Materials: FLASHCARDS

Snap

Snap is a traditional card game which can be played with word cards.

- Choose key words.
- Students make FLASHCARDS for the words if they do not already have them (SEE PAGE 54). They use one set each of the words for this.
- Place the students in groups or pairs.
- Students shuffle their cards. Holding their cards so that they can't see the words, the students take it in turns to put the cards face up on the table, one on top of the other.
- When two cards in sequence are the same, the first student to shout *Snap!* and the word on the FLASHCARD takes all the cards in the centre.
- As the students lose all their cards they are out. The last student with cards is the winner.

Happy Families

This can be played with any word family.

- Divide the class into groups of four or five students.
- Give four FLASHCARDS from a single word family to each member of the group, e.g. Child A has *cat, dog, lion* and *horse*; Child B has *bus, car, train* and *boat*; Child C has *milk, tea, orange juice, Coca-Cola*, and so on.
- The students look carefully at their cards, then all the cards for the group are mixed together and dealt out randomly to the students.
- Students have to recompose their word family by asking, in turn, for the cards they need, e.g. *Juan, have you got the bus?*
- The student who completes his/her word family first is the winner.

ACTIVITY 18: WORD CHAINS

Level: beginners/elementary

Aim: word recognition

Group dynamics: pairwork/individual

Language: classroom instructions, key vocabulary of your choice

---

- Using the key vocabulary, write on the board a number of words together in a 'chain' without any breaks. This can be done in the form of a snake, rope, road, etc. Write the key words at random around the chain as reference.
- Students copy down the chain and try to break the chain up into the individual words.

Adapting for higher levels

- Add letters in the chain between the words to make it more complicated.
- Or you can make the last letter of each word the first letter of the next, e.g. *bir(d)o(g)iraff(e)lephan(t)ige(r)abbi(t)ortoise.*

Which of these games could your students make for themselves to revise given word families? For example, one group can make the FLASHCARDS for another group. Choose a word family, show the students how to make the cards and tell them how many to make.

CHAPTER 8

Class management

In this chapter we shall look at some of the issues related to day-to-day classroom management. Managing the class successfully is fundamental to a successful classroom atmosphere for both you and your students.

Group dynamics

Traditionally, all classroom work was done using two basic forms of classroom dynamics.

- The teacher addressed the whole group, who responded in unison or one by one. This is known as 'frontal' teaching.
- The students were set work to do alone, usually on reading or writing tasks.

With only these two dynamics the time involved in **active** communication is extremely limited and sometimes non-existent. It is, perhaps, an attractive method for the teacher because discipline in the classroom is very easy and the students are quiet! However, if students are to learn to **speak** English, you will have to accept a certain amount of noise in the classroom.

Newer approaches to teaching languages offer us different possibilities of classroom dynamics which make class activities much more communicative and efficient.

Different GROUP DYNAMICS are particularly appropriate for certain tasks. Try to vary the dynamics that you use in each lesson to make your classes more lively.

The advantages of using different dynamics

- You will be able to provide your students with additional speaking time.
- We should never underestimate the value of the 'student teacher'. By allowing your students to work in pairs or small groups they develop their skills for passing information to each other. Weaker students benefit from the learning strategies being passed on by their peers and stronger students reinforce their learning by being placed in the position of having to explain language.
- When you first start teaching the younger primary students you will often find that their attitude to learning is highly egocentric and they are constantly demanding your individual attention. Pair or small groupwork makes students co-operate with each other and become more independent of the teacher.
- By organising the class into small groups or pairs you will be able to spend some time working individually with students who are having difficulties, either on their own or in small special groups.
- If your class has mixed abilities or mixed ages you will be able to set different groups different tasks, according to their abilities and ages.
- Younger students often need to move around **physically** during a lesson. If you try to make a group of eight year olds sit perfectly still in the same position throughout the lesson, you will almost certainly begin to experience discipline problems. By dividing your lessons into different group dynamics you allow for this need to stand up and move about.

Group dynamics

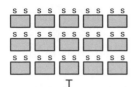

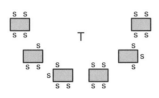

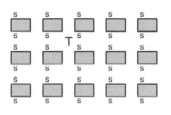

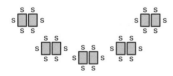

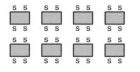

These are the most useful dynamics that you can try in your lessons.

Teacher to whole group

Useful for: presentation activities where the focus is on the teacher and the students are usually quiet.

Advantage: easy discipline.

Disadvantage: students' participation is limited to choral response or individually answering a direct question from the teacher.

Small groups

Useful for: communication activities, acting and project work. Walk around the classroom intervening occasionally in the groupwork.

Advantages: increased co-operation between students; more student autonomy.

Disadvantage: increased noise levels; you may need to exercise your authority to settle disputes between students.

Pairwork

Useful for: guided dialogues and ROLEPLAY. Set the task and then walk around checking and correcting. If it is difficult to walk around the classroom, arrange the pairs in such a way that you can supervise them from two or three points.

Advantage: all students get the opportunity to speak in class.

Disadvantage: not possible to check and correct all the mistakes.

Individual work

Useful for: writing exercises in the activity book where each student works alone. It should be preceded by some form of presentation to the whole class. Walk around correcting the students' work as they progress through the exercise.

Advantages: allows some quiet thinking time; changes pace and calms children down.

Disadvantages: more of a possibility that students might do a whole exercise incorrectly. Supervise the first part of the exercise quickly to avoid this. Students will not all work at the same pace. Always have some activities ready for the students who finish first.

Teacher to individual students

Useful for: checking the progress of a particular student.

Advantages: gives you the chance to get to know students; increases student's sense of belonging.

Disadvantages: too much teacher to individual work will become very boring for the rest of the class. Combine this with individual work so that while the class is working quietly on an activity you can attend to an individual student.

Small group to small group

Useful for: if the class have been working on an activity in small groups, they can be asked to contrast their work with another group.

Advantage: increases student autonomy.

Disadvantage: as the size of the groups gets bigger, so the noise level and the number of disputes increase!

Pair to pair

Useful for: personalised activities where the students can compare and contrast their ideas with those of another pair.

Advantages and disadvantages: as above.

47

Discipline

This is an extremely contentious area and you will probably find as many different opinions as to how to discipline students as there are teachers in the world! Ultimately you will have to decide on your own disciplinary rules for your classes. There are many different reasons why we experience discipline problems in our classrooms. The following is a basic guide for classroom management, detecting problems and applying remedies.

Classroom management

Noise

Do not expect primary school students to work in silence. It is normal for children to laugh and talk to each other while they are doing an activity. They want to know what their partner has done and, especially, who has finished first!

Rather than trying to prevent them from communicating normally with each other, prompt them to speak in English. Provide them with the language they need for this communication, e.g. *Have you finished? Look at my picture! Oh! That's pretty! What's that?* You can best do this by using this language yourself.

Movement

Children need to move around. The school day is long and we cannot reasonably expect them to sit at desks all day. Try to include at least one moving activity in each lesson. Let them stand up or clap and act to songs and rhymes.

Flexibility

Be prepared to change the order of your activities in your lesson plan to take into account the mood of your students. If they seem unruly at the beginning of the lesson, start off with a physical activity. If they get restless halfway through the lesson, stop what you are doing and get them moving.

Consistency

Be consistent. If your students know what you expect of them it will be easier for them to behave appropriately. This can be hard because as teachers we also have our good days and bad days! Do not expect students to be good always. Those of us who have children of our own know that their behaviour varies from day to day.

Fairness

Do not label children as 'difficult' just because they, or their brothers and sisters, have a history of disruptive behaviour. Try to show them that you have no preconceived ideas about them. If you allow children to think that you expect them to be naughty, you will, almost certainly, not be disappointed!

Positive reinforcement

Always emphasise and reinforce the good things that students do. Children love public encouragement, so make sure that the other students hear you praising and appreciating someone's work or conduct. Remember that all students need this praise, even the ones who do not always demand your approval. Never humiliate or use your advantages of age and experience to belittle a student no matter what they have done. Serious violations of the rules should always be dealt with privately.

Problems and remedies : This chart looks at the possible causes and remedies of disruptive behaviour.

PROBLEMS	REMEDIES
Boredom Disruptive behaviour is often a symptom of boredom.	The classwork may be too easy for the student(s). Try offering more of a challenge. The classwork may be too routine. Try more variety.
Passivity This may also be a symptom of boredom. On the other hand the student may feel out of his/her depth.	Try as above or spend some time with the individual student to help with specific problems. Try giving him/her responsibilities within the classroom, like helping other students.
Aggressive behaviour A student may be physically or verbally aggressive towards his/her classmates or even the teacher. This is usually a symptom of distress. The student may feel isolated by his/her classmates.	Try involving the students in activities which help him/her to integrate into a group. The student may be reproducing behavioural patterns learned at home. Check with other members of staff or the school psychologist. Aggressive behaviour can be a momentary reaction to a distressing situation like the loss of a member of the family. Try speaking to the student privately.
Stealing It is not uncommon for students to borrow things from their friends without asking. They often fail to identify this as stealing.	When you start the school year, make it clear that this kind of behaviour is not acceptable. Ask students to write their names clearly on all their things and spend time at the end of each lesson giving things back and putting things away. Discourage students from bringing expensive, tempting items to school. If necessary, send a letter to the parents at the beginning of the school year with a simple list of school materials. Ask them not to give their children a lot of money to bring to school.
Lying Young children often have a flexible idea of what is true and what is not. Do not confuse lying with fantasy. Lying is a deliberate manipulation of the facts in order to avoid responsibility or hurt another person. The rest is fantasy and is a natural feature of child behaviour.	If a student lies when asked if they are responsible for something, they may be doing this out of fear. Make sure that your relationship with your students is not based on fear.
Bullying Bullying is a form of aggressive behaviour which is often not immediately noticeable in the victims because they may well hide the truth from you for fear of being ignored by their classmates.	Bullying must be dealt with at once; it is harmful to both the victim and the bully. Observe the interaction between members of the class during groupwork and, if possible, in the playground. Look out for students picking on physical differences, such as a child wearing glasses or an obese child. Try groupwork and pairwork to encourage co-operation among the students. Deal with any severe cases with the help of other members of staff and/or the school psychologist.

Monitoring

Monitoring is essentially a task of programming and adapting continuously throughout the year according to the requirements of your students.

- Before you start the school year you should prepare your syllabus, based on your coursebook and any extra work you wish to include.
- Once you have taught the first few lessons you will begin to get an idea of how fast your students are likely to move and of the different abilities in your class. Adjust your programme accordingly. If you feel that the students need more time to practise the language presented in a unit, prepare extra activities to allow for this.

- After you have completed the first unit and have monitored the students' progress you can adjust your programme to take into account any deviations from the original plan. For example, you may decide that your students need fifteen hours' work on each new language item instead of the prescribed ten hours in your coursebook. This will mean that you may not be able to cover all the coursebook units in one academic year.

- On the other hand you may find that after a slow start your students begin to work faster. By monitoring their progress carefully you can be flexible with your programme.

Working with children

Try to build up a relationship with students based on **mutual** trust and respect.

- Avoid showing favouritism or negative attitudes towards certain children. Some do make it hard to like them! Try to overcome this by understanding that these children often need your approval even more than the others.

- Show care and understanding towards your students. If you see a student upset or distressed, take time off English, give the class something to do and spend time talking to him/her.

- Let students express their opinion in class and try to involve them in some decision making, e.g. *Which song shall we sing this afternoon?*

- Be prepared to accept a certain noise level in the classroom. Noise in itself is not a bad thing as long as it is productive. Prepare rules for the classroom (PAGE 32) and keep reminding the children of these if you fear an activity might get out of hand.

Eye contact

When you are doing oral work in the classroom, it often happens that one or two students tend to dominate oral work by shouting or talking over others. Try using eye contact to control the situation: by breaking eye contact deliberately while the student is speaking, we are indicating that we do not wish him/her to go on speaking or that we are not interested any more in what he/she has to say. This is a subtle way of controlling talking time among students. On some occasions you may find that a student carries on talking regardless. In this case you have no option but to ask him/her to be quiet and let somebody else speak for a change.

Trust

Trust is the essential element in the relationship between students and teachers. It is important to build up an atmosphere of trust and not to maintain authority by fear or threats, e.g. that a student may have to repeat the year if he/she 'doesn't behave'. Build up trust by getting to know the children, valuing their opinions, behaving fairly and consistently, and not expecting too much of them.

During a lesson in the near future, make notes on a piece of paper of a) the different dynamics you use during the lesson, and b) any discipline problems you have. Read through this chapter again and decide a) if you varied the dynamics enough and b) why your discipline problems arose.

CHAPTER 9

Lesson planning

If you are using a teacher's book, you will probably have suggested plans for all the lessons. These ready-prepared lesson plans are extremely useful for the day-to-day running of your class and they provide you with valuable time to spend on planning extra activities and monitoring your students' progress.

You should, however, be wary of simply following the lesson plans in the teacher's book: they are guides only. By introducing your own ideas, you make your classes much more lively for both you and your students.

Timing your lesson

Timing is an extremely important element of your lesson planning, so that you have neither too much nor too little work for each lesson. It will also help you to pace the activities so that all the students have time to finish each one satisfactorily.

The amount of time that each activity will take depends on a number of elements:

… the age of your students

… the degree of difficulty of the activity

… the end product of the activity (a written piece of work will always take more time)

In order to help you to plan your timing, try imagining each activity as being composed of these three parts.

Explaining the activity

You need time to make sure that all the children understand what they are expected to do. This will depend largely on the complexity of the activity. Some activities are almost self-explanatory, e.g. a matching exercise with a ready-drawn example, especially once the children are familiar with this type of exercise.

Performing the activity

The time needed to perform the activity will depend on what kind of end product is involved. Don't underestimate drawing and writing time.

Correcting the activity

Always take into account the time you need for checking the activity. This depends on the correction technique you choose and the length of the activity. It is important to make sure that you leave enough time to correct thoroughly. Correcting the work in the next lesson is never as successful because the children are already thinking about something else. ◆ SEE CHAPTER 13

The pace of your lesson

Not all your students will work at the same pace. Some finish activities very quickly while others need more time, particularly with written work. It is important that you allow enough time for all students to finish the core work. Rather than making slower students leave exercises unfinished, make sure that you have extra work for those who finish quickly. You can use simple activities like colouring in pictures, making a similar activity for a partner (e.g. puzzle-type activities), or have a selection of extra worksheets with reinforcement activities ready.

Many coursebooks now contain a certain number of graded exercises for you to use with faster students so they do not get bored in the classroom. Try to set aside special tasks for these students, by extending the exercise that everyone is doing or by giving them other things to do, e.g. continuing with a project, doing exercises from the activity book or reading a simplified reader.

Starting the class

Always remember to include a few minutes at the beginning of the lesson to settle the children down and quickly revise the key elements of the previous lesson. If your students are in a particularly boisterous mood, you could try doing some kind of physical activity. It is quite effective to establish a routine which has to be followed at both the beginning and end of all your lessons. This can be something as simple as taking it in turns to write the date on the board, handing out corrected work or, at the end, putting the chairs up on the table. Alternatively, you could establish that every class begins and ends with a song/rhyme and let the students choose the weekly programme.

Finishing the class

It is equally important to dedicate a few minutes at the end of each lesson to feedback and putting things away. This is when you ask the students to summarise what they have learned. You can also ask them to say which activities they most enjoyed and which activities they did not like, then to draw a smiley face next to the activities they liked, and a sad face next to the ones they did not like in their books.

Opposite is an example of a lesson plan. PHOTOCOPIABLE PAGE 7 provides an outline for reproducing this lesson plan for your lessons.

Let us imagine that we are going to present *Parts of the body* in a sixty-minute class. We shall plan the lesson to get an even balance between the following:

- aims of the lesson
- presentation/practice/recycling
- different group dynamics
- quiet and moving activities.

Analysis

Let's look at the lesson plan. The first thing was to establish the aims: the key language, sound, sociocultural activity; working out what we could recycle and making a note of the materials we needed.

We then planned our lesson to take into account the three elements of presentation, practice and recycling. The personalised activities fit in at any stage since they are a question of relating the language to the student.

The **presentation stage** moved from quiet individual work, listening and doing, to personalised pairwork. The **practice stage** moved from individual writing work to checking in groups and on to a whole-group rhyme which got the students moving. The **recycling stage** involved groupwork and a variety of skills.

We included different dynamics of groupwork and pairwork and tried to make sure that students alternated between quiet and moving activities.

At the end of each activity we estimated the time this activity would take and then worked out the total time. If our lesson time were less than 60 minutes, we would probably change the activity at the recycling stage for something which could be done faster, as suggested in the plan.

Plan your next lesson using PHOTOCOPIABLE PAGE 7. How did the timing work out? What adjustment do you have to make to your activities to fit them in better?

LESSON PLAN

Aim: Present and practice 'Parts of the body'.
Key vocabulary: Head, eyes, nose, ears, mouth, arms, legs, hands, feet
Pronunciation: /z/
Sociocultural activity: Rhyme: I've Got Two Eyes To Look Around
Recycling: Numbers 1-10 and the verb have got
Materials: Card, coloured paper, pencils, scissors, glue, assortment of dry food stuffs and packets, e.g. macaroni, rice, yoghurt pots, empty boxes from soap and toothpaste

STARTING THE CLASS

Tell students we are going to be working with the parts of the body.

Tell students to stand up. Demonstrate moving parts of the body: move first the head, then arms, legs, eyes, noses and mouths. Students copy. Tell students to move all their body and sit down.

Time: 3 minutes

PRESENTATION Parts of the body

Step 1: Use coursebook story. Students listen to the cassette and touch parts of the body on the picture in their coursebook, as they hear the words

Time: 6 minutes

Step 2: Check understanding: divide the class into pairs, play the cassette again and ask students to touch their partners on the part of the body they hear and say the word. Check and correct /z/.

Time: 6 minutes

PRACTICE

Step 1: Do matching exercise from the activity book with parts of the body and writing over the words. (The students that finish first can colour in the pictures.)

Time: 8-10 minutes

Step 2: Teach a rhyme about parts of the body. Students move while they are learning. They make gestures and facial expressions and move the parts of their bodies as they say the different words.

Time: 10-12 minutes

RECYCLING

Step 1: Collage of a creature from outer space
— Divide class into small groups. Give each group materials from above.
— Students design a creature with non-human features, e.g. six legs, three eyes ..., and give it a name.
— Students take it in turns to show and describe their creature to rest of the class e.g. SS: This is ... It has got six legs, three eyes ... (recycles have got and numbers)
Step 2: If time allows play a game with the collages. What am I describing? Students take it in turn to describe one of the creatures while the rest of the class works out which creature is being described.

Time: 20 minutes

FINISHING THE CLASS

Students draw sad/smiley face next to matching ex, then put away their things.

Time: 3 minutes

TOTAL TIME = 56-60 minutes

CHAPTER 10

Making simple resources

"What are the advantages of resources?"

Coursebooks are usually written for a variety of different situations and cannot take into account the many variations that exist in different schools, e.g.

- Numbers in the class. Coursebooks are generally written for classes of +/–25. In many rural areas the numbers are considerably lower, making many of the activities difficult to perform unless you adapt them.
- Mixed ability in the class. While most coursebooks now take this factor into account by offering extra exercises for fast finshers, the core of the book is written to a standard level.
- Availability of resources. Not all schools have the same facilities, particularly with respect to technology.
- Social environments. Differing social environments both limit and open new possibilities for the teacher, e.g. schools in cities can take children to the museum or even to the cinema to see films in English.
- Things of local interest. Many of the key vocabulary items can be enhanced with a little local flavour, e.g. food that is common in your area, wild animals and plants from your region will not necessarily be dealt with in a book designed for greater coverage. You could make FLASHCARDS of these items or add them to posters.

The great advantage of making and using your own resources is that you are able to take all of these factors into account and to tailor the classroom activities to suit your own particular environment and locality.

You can use resources in one of two ways.

- To reinforce something from the coursebook, e.g. in the form of games, puzzles, posters, wall charts, bulletin boards and so on.
- To introduce a cross-curricular element to your classwork.

Flashcards

On PAGES 11–15 we looked at the different components of the course materials and saw that in some cases there would be FLASHCARDS. If your course materials do not provide this resource, it would be advisable to think about making your own.

Decide on the size of card that your students will handle best. Generally speaking the younger the student, the bigger the card needs to be. Cards of $12 \times 8\,\text{cm}$ are a good, manageable size. You may need to alter the size of the card according to the use you will make of them in the classroom. For example, if you wish to use the FLASHCARDS for presentation of language from the front of the class, they will need to be bigger than if the students are to use them for practice in pairwork.

Identify the key language for the unit. You can make a card for each word or for a chosen number of words.

You can choose to make the cards using only illustrations, only words or illustrations and words. This will depend on the ability and age of your group. The younger the children, the less likely they are to respond to words only.

7–8 years

8–9 years

9–10 years

10–11 years

11–12 years

The illustrations can be drawn on or cut out of magazines and glued on. Sometimes the students' drawings are not very clear and this makes it difficult to use the cards. Perhaps you could use a combination, e.g. the FLASHCARDS for the colours could be drawn as circles of colours, but the parts of the body could be cut out of magazines. If you want the cards to last, it is a good idea to cover them with transparent plastic, although this makes them more expensive to produce.

"How can I use flashcards?" See the project on Letter Boxes on PAGE 60 and the card games on PAGES 44 AND 45. You could also use some of the following exploitation techniques.

1 Show and say
- Hold up a FLASHCARD and ask the class *What's this?*
- The students respond, e.g. *A banana.*
- Students can take turns in holding up the cards.

2 Find the pair
- Students work in pairs, each with a set of FLASHCARDS.
- They lay them face down on the table and take it in turn to turn over two cards trying to find a pair.
- The student that makes the most pairs is the winner.

3 Hide and seek
- Hide an agreed number of FLASHCARDS in the classroom.
- Write the words on the board as a guide.
- The students have to find the cards.
- When all the cards have been found the students stand up and say which cards they have. The student who finds the most cards is the winner.

4 Describe and guess
- Take a FLASHCARD from an agreed group of objects.
- Without showing it to the class, describe the object on the FLASHCARD.
- The class must guess which object is being described.

This is useful to revise adjectives, e.g. you might describe an apple as *a round fruit; it can be yellow, red or green*. The students can play this in groups.

5 Tell the story

- Choose a scene from a story.

- As you tell the story to the class, replace the key vocabulary with FLASHCARDS which you hold up. The students call out the missing words.

- Make sure that the key vocabulary is repeated and see if the students can anticipate the missing word before you hold up the FLASHCARD.

Posters

Visual examples of language are very important in the primary school classroom. Posters, which you can make yourself or in class as part of a group activity, are useful visual resources. You can keep them in a box if necessary, taking them to class now and again for revision work. Here are two examples of posters.

Collages

- Choose your key language.

- Students look through old magazines for examples of the key language and glue them onto card, making an abstract design, e.g. for colours, you could have one poster for each colour. Different groups work with different colours and produce, e.g. *A Yellow Poster* comprising things which are yellow, etc.

- To make the posters more attractive, mount them on black card and put them up on the wall.

Information boards

- Choose your key language.

- Students work in groups collecting and displaying information on their poster, e.g. *wild animals*. Each group is given or chooses a different wild animal. Give all the groups a set of defined tasks, e.g.
  1 Where does this animal live?
  2 What does this animal eat?
  3 Describe your animal.

- Make sure you give enough language examples on the board.

- Mount posters on black card and put up on them up on the wall.

Friezes

These are long illustrations which can be displayed at the top or bottom of the wall. They are usually used to display language in context, e.g. a farm. For this frieze, students can just have pictures and words as labels or they can use language bubbles to display key structures.

- Students work in groups, each group responsible for a part of the frieze.
- Use a long strip of white lining paper, approximately ½m × 2m, coloured paper, paints, glue and scissors.
- Plan the frieze with the class and decide what you are going to put on it.
- One group should be responsible for the background, e.g. in the case of the farm, painting the fields, pond, road, hills ...
- Other groups make cut outs and glue them onto the frieze in an appropriate place, e.g. they put the cows in a field.
- When it is finished, mount it on the wall and use it for language practice.

Friezes can also be used to illustrate songs and stories. The example above could be done as an illustration to the song *Old MacDonald Had a Farm*.

This chapter contains a limited number of activities which you can try. However, the best resources will be those you make to suit your own situation. Consider the following as a guide to making your own resources.

- What language area I am trying to teach?
- Which skill(s) do I want the students to use?
- Which dynamic(s) do I want to use in the activity? (pairwork, small groups, individual)
- How long do I want to spend on this activity?
- What kind of activities in the coursebook and activity book do my students get the most out of? (matching exercises, word puzzles, acting games)
- How much student language can I involve in this activity?
- What materials do I need to prepare for this activity?
- Can I use it again in the future?
- Do any teachers from other subject areas have material I can use?

Look at the next two or three units in your coursebook. Identify a topic which will interest your students and work out some resources which you can make with the class, e.g. information posters or a frieze.

CHAPTER 11

Projects

Cross-curricular activities in the form of projects are very useful for:

... bringing together several disciplines in the classroom
... extending students' interest in and knowledge of English
... helping students to see English as a vehicle with a purpose
... developing students' autonomy and independence from the teacher.

When working with projects you may find it useful and interesting to co-ordinate the English input with other subjects. Particular subjects offer different possibilities for linking up with the English programme, e.g.

- Art: This is always used in the presentation of project work, but you might like to check with the art teacher about specific work such as primary, secondary and tertiary colours and do some work on this in the English class.

- Music: The mini-project on PAGE 60 offers a clear link with music studies. If your students are making instruments in their music class, you could use these for percussion in class when they have learned a new song.

- History: Children are often fascinated by colourful characters in history like Alexander the Great, Ghengis Khan and many of the explorers. These characters offer you wonderful scope for mini-projects, especially if you want to practise the past tense. Don't forget to include some women!

- Geography: Most children are working with regional geography at the primary stage. A project can link with regions and geographical features like rivers and mountain ranges.

- Science: At primary school, science studies tend to include the observation of the basic physical principles and the developing of environmental awareness. A suitable project might be a recycling programme in which students have to collect and weigh paper for recycling.

You could either do a specialised project linking up with one of these projects or try a full-scale project which will involve many different subject areas.

Let us imagine that we are going to do a project on food and health. We shall separate the project into three stages: planning, research, and presentation.

Project plan: food and health

Planning

- Having decided on the subject area of the project, look for possible links with other school subjects, in this case science, history and geography.

- Divide the subject of the project up into a number of different parts. Use the information you have obtained from the other teachers about the work the children are covering in other subjects to help you set the different tasks, e.g.

  ... different elements in food (vitamins, carbohydrates ...)
  ... food from around the world
  ... food that is good for you and food that is not
  ... food from animals and food from plants
  ... different colours in food (no food is blue!)
  ... different eating habits in different countries
  ... food to go with different seasons of the year and different weather
  ... different forms of food packaging (tins, packets, tubes ...).

Choose the elements according to the age of your students and any cross-curricular considerations.

- Decide how the different elements will be presented or displayed. You can choose from the following.

  Posters. These are simple illustrations of different food with the names written underneath.

  Bulletin boards. These are more sophisticated than posters and contain a variety of information like labels from food products, recipes, packets of seed for growing food and so on.

  Information charts. These display information in a very visual way.

  Table displays. These consist of food products placed on a table with cards next to each object explaining something interesting about the food.

  Plays and roleplays. These can be used to show how important food is to our everyday living.

  Maps. These show where food comes from.

  Questionnaires. These are particularly good for stimulating communication.

- Divide the class up into groups and make each group responsible for a different element of the project. Tell the students which presentation they should do.

Research

- Each group now researches its area using reference books, maps, dictionaries, encyclopaedias, magazines and so on. This work can be done both in class and after class, either at home or in the school library. Make sure that students know exactly what they are expected to produce and that each member of the team has a clear set of instructions. Make sure that each group has a box to keep all their materials in, e.g. a shoe box.

- Students bring their information, REALIA, etc. to the class. In their groups, they design their part of the project and write in rough any accompanying texts/labels. Give the students language models and then correct the rough version before they transcribe it onto their final display.

Presentation

- Once the work is completed, the project can be displayed in the form of an exhibition. Set a date for your exhibition and ask each group to stand by its exhibit and be prepared to offer explanations about it. If one of the groups is going to perform a small play or a ROLEPLAY, set a time for the performance so that everybody stops to watch. Ask an audience to come and see the project. This may be students and teachers from other classes, or even parents.

"What happens if students use L1?"

All project work will involve a certain amount of L1 while the children are working in groups, and you may have to clarify certain points in L1 to make sure that they understand what to do. Follow the guidelines on PAGE 33 for use of L1 in class and remember to reinforce English as you walk around supervising groupwork.

"How long does it take to do a project?"

Project work is very time-consuming and requires a lot of preparation. It is, however, very rewarding for both teachers and students. Projects like the one described above will take several lessons. You can reserve either one lesson a week or a certain amount of time each lesson until the project has been completed.

Mini-projects

You can also do mini-projects, which will take up less time and cover a much more limited field. Here are three ideas for mini-projects offering extension work on letters, sounds and words.

MINI-PROJECT 1: LETTER BOXES

Level: beginners

Aim: to store words in alphabetical order (an ongoing activity)

Group dynamics: whole group/small groups

Language: alphabet, classroom instructions

Materials: 26 shoe boxes with their lids (ask the students to bring them in – different sizes will be fine), paints, scissors, FLASHCARDS

This activity is designed to introduce the idea of storing words in alphabetical order. It is a pre-dictionary activity. It could be used at the end of each lesson when the students store the key words they have learned. Store the boxes where the students can refer to them but make a point of checking them after use or they will get in a terrible mess! If you do not have an English classroom, ask each student in the class to take responsibility for one box.

- Paint the shoe boxes and cut a slot in the lid which is long enough for FLASHCARDS to slip through.
- Paint each letter of the alphabet onto a different box.
- Use for storing FLASHCARDS according to the initial letter of the card/picture.

Other activities

To use the letter boxes in class you could try the following games.

- The posting game: each team/student has to post their FLASHCARDS.
- Empty the letter boxes, mix the FLASHCARDS up and ask the students to sort them out into the correct boxes.
- Mix up the lids of the boxes, ask students to look at the FLASHCARDS in the boxes and find the right lids.

MINI-PROJECT 2: THE SOUND PIANO

Level: beginners

Group dynamics: whole group/small groups

Aim: to maintain an ongoing emphasis on sounds in English

Language: classroom instructions, English sounds

Materials: a sheet of white paper 2 × 1m

This project is an ongoing activity which will take several months or even a whole school year to complete. It is a good idea to set aside a standard time for this so that students know when they will be doing the activity and may be encouraged to participate and co-operate on their own initiative.

Each key on the piano represents a vowel sound. Work with **one** sound over a period of time, e.g. one every two weeks. If your course provides pronunciation work, follow the pattern in the book; if not, here is the full list of vowel sounds:

/iː/ be /ɪ/ big /e/ head /æ/ black /ɑː/ car /ɒ/ stop /ɔː/ your
/ʊ/ look /uː/ blue /ʌ/ cut /ə/ mother /ɜː/ girl /eɪ/ name /aɪ/ like
/ɔɪ/ boy /əʊ/ nose /aʊ/ mouth /eə/ chair /ɪə/ here /ʊə/ sure

This activity allows for variations depending on your class work, e.g. with younger children, reduce the number of vowel sounds and keys on the piano; if you wish to include consonants, make another sound piano.

- On the long sheet of paper draw a piano keyboard with seven white keys and five black keys for the simple long and short vowel sounds, or extend to twelve white keys and eight black keys to use the diphthongs too, e.g.

Simple sound piano   More complex one

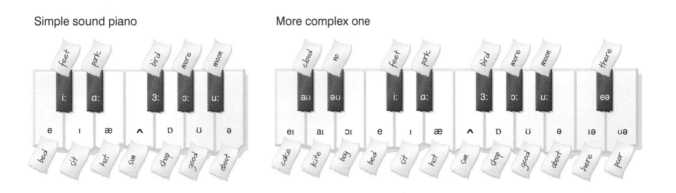

- Distribute the sounds along the black and white keys by writing an example of a word with that sound.
- After you have practised the sound in class, ask the students to make small word/picture cards and to glue them on to the appropriate key on the piano.

This project can be incorporated into cross-curricular music studies.

MINI-PROJECT 3: THE ENGLISH FRIEZE

Level: beginners/elementary

Group dynamics: whole group/small groups

Aim: to make an English frieze

Language: classroom instructions

Materials: a long sheet of white paper approximately 1 × 2m, glue, magazines, newspapers, printed material

---

- Ask the students to look through comics, magazines, trade marks, labels on food packets and clothing, instructions on compact disc players, radios, etc. and either cut out or write down words which they think are English.
- Check all the words, and discuss where they came from and what the students think they mean by using the context. Do this in L1 to encourage them to use their initiative.
- Glue the words on the frieze to form a collage.
- Encourage students to keep on bringing in more English words and building on the frieze.

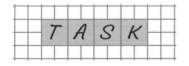

Think about how you can exploit one of the projects or mini-projects for classroom activities once the children have finished making it. How can you use it for language practice? Can you make a game out of it?

CHAPTER 12

Stories, plays, songs and rhymes

All of these are of enormous value in the primary classroom as they are more than just simple vehicles of language. They offer us the opportunity to convey social elements for child development. Children will often forget linguistic inhibitions when acting or singing, and activities used with songs, stories, etc. can help to foster co-operation in class. Don't worry too much if the children use L1 when preparing the activities below; they are working towards an end product in English.

Stories

Using traditional children's stories

If your coursebook does not have stories, you could use your own stories. Be wary of simply reading out a story from an English children's book, as you will almost certainly have to simplify the language.

The story does not have to contain only language that the children already know, in fact it is better if there is a more natural flow to the story, but you must include key language that will help them to follow the story. Use plenty of facial expression, voice expression and gestures as well as pictures to put the language into context.

Remember that all children's stories must contain a lot of repetition. For example, imagine you are telling the class the story of *Jack and the Beanstalk*. When you come to the part where the beanstalk is growing, repeat the lines and ask the students to join in:

T: *And the beanstalk got bigger and bigger and bigger and bigger!*

T/C: *And the next day, the beanstalk got bigger and bigger and bigger and bigger!*

The children join in with *bigger and bigger*; it does not matter that they have not seen the past tense of *get*: with pictures and gestures they will follow the story.

You may need to alter the story slightly for your purposes, for example in the real story of *Jack and the Beanstalk*, the beanstalk grows overnight, but for repetition purposes you can let it grow over several days. Be careful, however, about changing critical parts because the students may become confused. If you try to change Jack's giant into a man from outer space, they will soon tell you you have got the story wrong!

Finally, remember that many traditional stories offer role models belonging to the past. You may need to change some of the characters' behaviour to offer more modern values. You will almost certainly need to change some of the characters to girls or to change the girls' behaviour in the story so that they are not always represented as the weaker sex.

Exploiting stories

The exploitation of a story in the classroom should cover several lessons. Do not worry about repetition, the children love it! However, you could try a slightly different approach each time. The following is an example of how you might exploit a story from your coursebook.

Picture observation

The story will probably be presented in picture form and may or may not have written language. In the first instance, forget the words if there are any and forget the story in itself. Concentrate on the pictures. Try following this order.

- Identify. Ask the students to identify elements in the pictures which they are familiar with, such as colours, numbers, objects, characters: *What colour is the tree? Count the houses. Tell me the names of the things in the garden.*

- Deduce. Ask the students to deduce from their observations: *Look at the tree. Why is Joey wearing a coat? What season of the year is it?*

- Give an opinion. Ask the students to express their opinion: *Do you like Joey's coat? Which house do you like best?*

You could then do extension activities based on these ideas. Try asking the students to memorise one of the pictures and then to draw it. They can then compare their drawing with their partner.

Listening to the story

The students are now ready to listen to the story. It is important to set the mood: ask the students to sit quietly and listen to the story. You may pin up the poster for the story if one is provided. If not, the students can look at their coursebook pictures. Should you find that the story is not on the cassette or you prefer to use one of your own stories, read the story yourself to the class. Ask them not to interrupt you.

Play the story all the way through at least twice, then do the activities in the coursebook or try some of the following.

- Read key sentences or phrases corresponding to each picture but not in the right order. The students have to identify which picture the sentence belongs to.

  T: *Oh dear! Joey is very frightened of the ghost. Which picture?*
  Class: *Number 3.*

- Read key sentences or phrases but make an obvious change. The students have to correct you.

  T: *Oh dear! Joey is very frightened of Mary. What's wrong?*
  Class: *Joey is frightened of the ghost.*

- Play 'Who said'. Read out a speech from the story. Ask the students to identify the speaker.

  T: *Who said, 'I'm frightened'?*
  Class: *Joey.*

63

- Read out the story, missing out one of the pictures. The students have to tell you which picture is missing.
- Read out the story and change the ending.
- Ask the students to make up another ending.
- Read out the story missing out some key sentences. The students call out the key sentences. Younger students particularly like this when the sentence is repetitive.

Acting out the story

Once you are satisfied that your students know the story well, you could try asking them to act it out in small groups. If your students have very limited language, just ask them to mime the story as you play the tape. If, on the other hand, you feel they are ready to try some of the text, ask them to learn a few lines each and act out the story. You could use puppets for the characters in the story. (For more ideas on stories, see *DEVELOPING RESOURCES FOR PRIMARY*, in the same series.)

Plays

Putting on a play

If you wish to use this technique once the students are familiar with a story, try the following procedure.

Planning

- Divide the class up into actors and organisers.
- If you don't have exactly the right number of students in the class, explain that all plays involve more people than just the actors. Introduce them to the other roles involved and choose the number of roles that you need in order to give everybody something to do. If you intend to do more than one performance in the year, vary the roles of each student so that they all have the opportunity to act and organise, but do not force any child to be on stage.

  The organising roles are: director   prop designer   costume designer   choreographer   prompter   script writer   music director (and lighting if the performance will be on a stage)   scenery artists   programme artists

  Give the students their official titles, it sounds important!

Preparation

- If you are going to use costumes and props you will have to supervise carefully. Make sure that it is kept **simple**. Masks are a good way of characterising animals and other non-humans. Children can use the cut-out on PHOTOCOPIABLE PAGE 8 and paint each mask according to the character. Glue on things like whiskers and hair for extra effect.

- For props, suggest children use portable objects like walking sticks, glasses, hats, bags. The students responsible for these areas should write out lists for each character in English and make sure that everything is ready for the performance.

- Scenery can be made by drawing on long white paper and pinning or taping this onto the backdrop. ◆ SEE PAGE 6

Rehearsal

- Let the different working groups organise themselves and give them rehearsal time. You will need to walk around supervising and reinforcing English whenever you can. You need to have a good idea of the script in order to set the children working on their individual and group tasks.

- The children who are acting should work with the director and prompter and sit and practise their lines until they are ready to rehearse on stage. The choreographer should mark movements on the script. These will be adapted once they start to practise on stage.

- The prop designer and costume designer should make lists of props and costumes needed for each scene while the scenery artists draw scenery on paper to be glued to the backdrop for each scene. Make sure that there are not too many scenes and that the children's plans are not too ambitious!

- The music and lighting directors should work out pieces of music they want to use and make tapes or decide which music they want from the class cassette. Lighting usually involves just switching the lights on and off at the appropriate times.

- The programme artists design a programme for the performance.

This will, obviously, take longer than just one lesson. Try dividing it up over a period of time, setting aside 20 minutes now and again as rehearsal time. It is not practical to try and do more than one play of this nature per term. Try making it an end-of-term activity, ready for a performance on the last day of school, when it is always difficult to teach!

Production

- Try to get together an audience of other students and teachers or even parents.

- For an end-of-term production, you could also include some songs or rhymes from your coursebook in the script.

Finally, do not be too ambitious. A simple ten-minute performance takes a lot of organising and is long enough for an audience that may not know English.

Songs and rhymes

Exploiting songs and rhymes

It is important to remember that songs and rhymes are about how English sounds. It is not a good idea to try and dissect the meaning of every word because you will destroy the natural rhythm of the verse. You might try this approach.

- Play the cassette to the class. Ask the children if they like the song.

- Play the cassette a second time and ask them to hum the tune.

- Play the cassette a third time, stopping after each line or verse. Rewind and play again asking the children to sing along with you.

- Repeat each verse several times. If the song is very long, consider doing it in two parts or even omitting some of the verses.

- Don't be tempted to write the words up on the board and don't ask the children to sing while reading from their coursebooks.

Repeat the song/rhyme over several classes and once you think the children know it well, try some of these activities.

Rounds

- Divide the class into groups of four or five students. Tell them that each group will start the song/rhyme at a different time.
- Point to the first group, who begins to sing/recite.
- Once they have completed the first line, the second group starts while the first group goes on to the second line.
- While the first group sings/recites the third line, the second group the second, the third group begins with the first line and so on until all the groups are singing/reciting.

The object of this exercise is to make the students concentrate on what they themselves are singing and not on the other students.

Singing competitions

- Once your students know several songs and rhymes, divide the class into groups as before.
- Each group chooses a song or rhyme from their book and performs it for the rest of the class.
- You can record the performance on the cassette recorder if you wish.
- After all the performances, the class votes on their favourite by writing the name of the song/rhyme they most enjoyed on a slip of paper.
- Collect the slips of paper and declare the winner.
- The winning group performs once again.

What's the missing word?

- Divide the class into groups.
- Each group chooses a song/rhyme and performs it for the rest of the class. However they miss out the last word in each line.
- When they come to the missing word they stop singing/reciting and the rest of the class has to call out the missing word.

Forfeits

- When you first meet your class, you can explain that if a student breaks the rules, he/she will have to perform a forfeit.
- In this case they must recite a short rhyme or sing a short song for the rest of the class.
- It is important to include the possibility of a rhyme because not all students feel comfortable about singing on their own in public.

Note: Make sure that this is done in a lighthearted way; you do not want the children to associate singing with punishment.

Look at the songs and rhymes in your coursebook for the year. Do you think that the students will like these songs? Can you think of others that they would prefer? Can you think of other ways of exploiting songs and rhymes?

CHAPTER 13

Correction techniques

"Why do students make mistakes?"

There are a number of reasons why students make mistakes:

... failure to study
... lack of understanding of a linguistic rule
... confusion with L1
... translating directly from L1
... trying to use words or structures which have not been covered in class.

"What should I correct?"

Understanding the different reasons for mistakes can help you to determine which ones to correct and how to correct them. For example, a consistent structural error may arise from lack of understanding, in which case you'll need to present the concept again; or confusion with L1, so some contrast work may be needed.

Oral work

Teacher correction

It can be difficult to determine how often and how much to correct oral work. Too much correction inhibits the students and too little means that they will learn incorrect language which is difficult to change later on. We have to try and strike a balance in the classroom between ACCURACY and FLUENCY. On the one hand our task is to teach our students correct English (ACCURACY), and on the other hand we want to motivate and stimulate our students into free expression (FLUENCY). For example, when practising the present simple, you will probably correct all errors with the tense but may overlook a pronunciation error.

Correcting students when they are working within the defined framework of an exercise is relatively simple since you have the aim of the exercise to use as a guideline. Difficulties arise when the students are working in a less defined area, e.g. acting out a story. In this case ask yourself *What can I reasonably expect my students to know well?* If your students are trying hard to express themselves with language of a higher level than you would normally expect, concentrate on their ability to communicate. If, on the other hand, they are making mistakes which they should not be making at this stage, then you should correct them.

Try to apply your correction criteria according to your expectations for individual students. Some need lots of encouragement to speak freely and should not be over-corrected but quicker students may benefit from a little more correction.

You will also find if you are working with large groups that it is too time-consuming to correct everything. Learn to accept mistakes and deal with them within the defined frameworks of the exercises as described above.

It is not a good idea to interrupt a performance of a ROLEPLAY, story, play or song to correct students. Wait until the end, taking notes as you detect errors and go through the mistakes with the whole class. It is not necessary to point out who made the mistake, just write the mistakes up on the board and ask the whole class if they can correct them.

Since being corrected can be a frustrating experience for students, try playing a game where they are allowed to correct you. This will take the stigma out of being corrected.

- Choose an oral drill that the students have just practised.
- Tell the students that you are now going to do the drill, but that they must listen very carefully because you are tired and you will certainly make some mistakes. When they hear a mistake they have to stand up and correct you.
- Perform the drill, making mistakes in the key structures or pronunciation, e.g. *I likes chocolate. He likes potatoes.* (pronounced *potato-es* /pəˈteɪtəʊes/)
- Ask the students to give you the correct form.
- This game can be extended by letting the students play the role of the teacher making deliberate mistakes. The rest of the class give the correct form. The advantage with this method is that in order to make the deliberate mistake the students must know the correct form.

Self correction and peer correction

Students often make errors in speech because of lapses of concentration or habit. In these cases, the student can often correct him/herself. You can signal by a facial expression that a student has made an error, and he/she can then try to correct it. If he/she can't correct the error, ask if any other students can.

You can also try peer correction by asking the students to identify errors as their classmates speak, and to correct them. Don't encourage the students to continuously interrupt each other, however. Remember that you are applying the correction criteria that we have described above and you should try to ensure that students pick up on relevant errors. If you are not careful, some quicker students may abuse peer correction to dominate weaker students and this is more demotivating than being corrected by you. Peer correction has the great advantage, though, of encouraging students to rely on each other rather than the teacher.

Written work

It is extremely important to remember that all the written work that you set your students should be checked and fully corrected. Let's look at some of the different approaches we can use for correcting written work.

Teacher correction

A standard technique is where you correct your students' books. This can be done after or during class. If possible, do this during class with the students present, as this is a more immediate approach to correcting and provides better results.

It is often preferable to write comments in the student's book rather than a simple mark. Remember that you can use these comments as an informal reading exercise as all students like to know what their teacher has written. These remarks should be personal, encouraging and humorous rather than disparaging. Try the following:

> *Super work, (student´s name)!*
> *Well done, (student´s name)!*
> *I like this picture very much, (student´s name).*
> *This is not your best work, (student´s name)!*
> *Oh dear, (student´s name)!*

Try to avoid comments that could be interpreted as marks, like *Excellent, Very good* or *Poor*, because they are not personal and may promote unhealthy competition in the classroom. If you keep a record of the comments, they can be very useful when it comes to evaluating your students. ◆ SEE CHAPTER 14

As an alternative to correcting the work yourself, try one of the following.

- Make a copy of the exercise, complete it and hand out completed copies to students. They correct their friend's work.

- If the exercise is not too long, you could write the correct answers on the board and ask the class to exchange books and correct each other's work.

- Correct the exercise orally with all the class and ask them to correct their own work or their neighbour's work.

Peer correction

An interesting alternative is to involve the students in the correction process. Pairwork is excellent for peer correction and offers you the possibility of using a different one of the four skills for correcting the work.

The advantages of peer correction are considerable.

- There is the practical advantage of having the students entertained in the task of correcting each other's work, giving you time to walk around checking and supervising.

- The task of identifying and understanding what is incorrect implies that the student knows what is right. This is an excellent method for you to check who has understood the exercise and who has not.

- The exchange of knowledge between students is a valuable form of teaching. Students will often explain and teach their peers structures using techniques which are well accepted by children. They may well teach their peers strategies for remembering a grammar rule that you would never think of.

Try using peer correction first in pairs as it is easier to manage. However, remember that students may not correct each other's work correctly! You should either provide the correct answers on the board or walk around checking. Although this may seem to involve two stages of correction, we should remember that peer correction is not just a correction technique, but it is also a learning stage. This correction technique can be used in exercise writing but not for free writing.

Peer correction can also be done in groups.

- Each group exchanges its books for correction by another group.

- Let the students discuss and disagree over the work in their own language while they are correcting. The advantage of this variation is that the correction technique is an extension of the activity.

Self correction

Some course materials have books with answers or a key. In this case the students can correct their own work. This is probably the least successful of all the techniques because students rarely see their own mistakes and you do not give them the advantage of a contrasting opinion. However, it is vital to insist the students check their work before it is handed in – which is in itself a form of self correction.

Make a note of the different correction techniques you use over the course of two weeks. Which were the most successful? Do any of the correction techniques work particularly well with a specific kind of task?

CHAPTER 14

Evaluation techniques

Assessment of your students' progress is essential for your preparation and programming. At primary level we are not concerned with our students learning a lot in terms of quantity of vocabulary and numbers of structures. Rather, we aim to provide them with small quantities of material that they will gradually build on and learn to use in a variety of situations. It is important to remember that we are concentrating primarily on developing the students' listening and speaking skills. For this reason, traditional tests consisting of gap-filling exercises or conjugating verbs are of little use to us.

Making an assessment plan

When preparing your assessment plan you should bear in mind the following.

- Your assessment should be made up of four basic testing areas:

  … CONTINUOUS ASSESSMENT of classwork and any homework
  … oral tests
  … written tests
  … general attitude and effort.

- You should always take into account individual abilities. If you only use written tests, it is difficult to take into account the different abilities in your class. One of the advantages of using a mixed assessment strategy is that you can encourage the students who have difficulties in English by rewarding good general work done in the classroom.

- Assessment should be often and in small quantities. Don't forget the age of your students: they learn quickly but they also forget quickly! It is a good idea to test again and again throughout the year. Give small mini-tests on specific language areas as you finish teaching them.

Continuous assessment

Each teacher has his/her own method for keeping track of classroom progress, though it is sometimes difficult to know how to assess this. The following is a suggestion you might like to try if you have not yet developed your own system.

- Keep a record book throughout the school year in which you make notes of each student's progress on a regular basis, e.g. at the end of each teaching unit or twice a term.

- Use descriptive criteria rather than numbers, e.g. *excellent progress, satisfactory progress, unsatisfactory progress*. By keeping the categories down to a small number, it is easier for you to establish your mark.

- Use simple definitions for each category, e.g.

  Excellent progress means that the student has understood and is able to use the language area covered without any difficulty at all. Be especially strict about applying this category: remember that if you use it too freely, you will not be able to stimulate good students to work even harder.

  Satisfactory progress means that the student has understood the language area and can use it relatively well but will still be making some mistakes. The vast majority of your class should fall into this category. Remember to take into account personal abilities. For some students, *satisfactory progress* represents a tremendous effort, but not for others.

Unsatisfactory progress means that a student is not keeping up with the general rhythm of the class and has not understood or learned the language covered. If you have more than just a few students in this category, you should take a good look at how you are delivering the class. Too many failures in one class means that the teacher is doing something wrong!

Recording marks

The process of CONTINUOUS ASSESSMENT involves marking students' written work on a regular basis. We have discussed some of the possible techniques for correcting in Chapter 13, but a record should be kept of the marks. You may find it easier to do this by using a straightforward technique like awarding marks out of ten for each exercise. Keep your own record of these marks and transform them into averages when you are making your assessment; it is not necessary to write numbers on the students' work. You can then interpret these marks in the way described above, e.g.

Excellent progress: Average marks = 8–10/10

Satisfactory progress: Average marks = 5–8/10

Unsatisfactory progress: Average marks = 0–5/10

See PHOTOCOPIABLE PAGE 9 for an example of an assessment sheet that you can use for your end-of-term assessments.

Oral tests

The most difficult part of learning a foreign language is learning to speak it. Most students will produce better results in a written test than in an oral test. This type of assessment is probably the most recent and therefore the least covered in courses. Oral testing is problematic from the organisational point of view.

"How can I organise oral tests?"

- Always tell the children that you are going to test them.
- Test them in small groups of about six. You will probably not have time to test them individually.
- Award the same mark to the whole group in order to stimulate the faster students into helping the slower ones.
- Each time you test, change the members of the groups around so that the children have to learn to work with different members of the class. However, make sure that each group is of a balanced mixed ability.
- Use different activities for testing, particularly activities that you know your class enjoys. For example, some of the games in your coursebook may be ideal for oral testing.
- Acting out small plays based on a story or a ROLEPLAY from the unit is ideal for oral testing because the children can move around.
- Remember to notice the non-linguistic elements that the children use in order to enhance communication, e.g. facial expressions, gestures and survival techniques like miming. This is language development and should be assessed. When a child accompanies verbal expression with an appropriate facial expression or gesture, this shows clear understanding of the language used. When he/she is not able to remember a word but can make himself/herself understood by using mime, this is a survival technique which while not quite as good as knowing the word is, nevertheless, an important part of language learning.

Written tests

This is the standard form of testing which you are probably familiar with from your own schooldays and which you may have to do with your students.

"How can I make written tests more relevant to my teaching?"

- Give children a choice of exercises, e.g. they have to do three exercises out of five. In this way they will have to read through all the exercises and choose. This in itself is a good language exercise!
- Do not make the children work too quickly. Give them plenty of time and insist on their checking work well before they hand it in. Check that they have understood the instructions in their own language.
- Include a *Listen and draw* or *Listen and write* exercise, as below.

Listen and draw

1 Read out a short text while the students follow the instructions, e.g. *Draw a **big table**. There is a **book on** the table and a **pencil under** the table. To the **left** of the table there is a **chair**. An **old man** is **sitting** on the chair. Now colour your picture.*

2 Award a point for each key word (in bold in the example). In this case there would be eleven marks in all for the exercise.

Listen and write

1 Write out a short text with words missing or with a choice of two words in key positions.

2 Give a copy of the text to each student.

3 Read out the completed text while the students write the missing word or underline the correct one, e.g. *Bobby and Jane are in the (kitchen/**sitting room**). They are (**watching**/looking at) TV. Bobby is wearing (**jeans**/shorts) and Jane is wearing a (blue/**red**) dress ...*

4 Award a point for each key word.

- Do not make the exercises too long. Four or five questions on each of the points you wish to assess is more than enough.
- Make sure that the children have some colouring in to do so that their exam paper looks more attractive.
- Collect all written tests and keep them till the end of term. At the end of term, let the children make a folder for their tests, which they can decorate as they like and take their tests home. Their parents will be pleased to see some of the work they have done.

General attitude and effort

It is not easy to assess your students' attitude and effort since it requires subjective criteria. In order to assess attitude we could consider the following points.

- Does this child participate freely in class?
- Does this child present his/her work well?
- Does this child co-operate well with his/her peers?
- Does this child perform all or most of the tasks set?

If you are answering *no* to some or all of these questions, try to consider why this might be the case.

- Is the child noticeably behind the general level of the group?
- Does this child have any physical or social difficulties which affect his/her work?

- Is this child having difficulty in integrating into the social group? (Does he/she have any friends? Is he/she left out when the students are choosing partners?)

Before you assess this child negatively, see if it is possible to correct some of the obstacles to his/her development. For example, it is not at all unusual for a child who is performing badly when sitting at the back of the class to improve when he/she is moved nearer to the front. It may be something as simple as not being able to see the board well enough.

If, in spite of this, you feel that you must assess a student's attitude as negative, try to be constructive in your assessment. Offer suggestions as to how this student might be stimulated into improving his/her attitude.

Effort is very individual. Take into account that students will each be applying different levels of effort to their work depending on:

… their interest in the subject

… their ability as students.

As teachers it is one of our main tasks to ensure that our students are interested enough in our classes to want to work hard and apply themselves. We do, however, have to take into account that some students need only limited effort to keep up with the general standard of the class while others need to exercise considerably more effort to achieve similar or even poorer results. When assessing effort, remember that the students who are obtaining the best marks are not necessarily applying more effort than the rest of the class, it is just that their effort goes a long way.

Effort is very much a question of need. Students will apply the amount of effort needed to perform the task before them to the standard that they think you require. If you feel that there is not much effort involved in their work, try gradually demanding a little more from them by increasing the difficulty of the work you set them. On the other hand, if you demand too much from a student who is struggling, you may find that he/she simply stops making any effort whatsoever. In this case, limit your expectations and be prepared to praise small achievements often. Emphasise the elements in the student's work that you are happy with and encourage him/her to carry on.

Guidelines for testing

Having seen a breakdown of assessment technique we must still bear in mind that for many students tests are very traumatic and they may perform below their ability, while others adopt an apathetic attitude, particularly in subjects which seem of no apparent value to the student.

"How can I prepare my students for tests?"

- Tell the students when they are going to have a test.
- Explain exactly what the students will be expected to do in the test so that they can revise. Tell them this again just before the test.
- Make sure that they understand the instructions well. Written instructions should be very similar to those used in the coursebook and activity book if they are not in L1. Many students fail to produce satisfactory work because they simply haven't understood.
- Test often and in small quantities. For example, if a unit has ten words of key vocabulary and one main structure, first test the students on the key vocabulary. A few days later test them on the structure, using the key vocabulary in the exercises. Don't try and do the two things together.

- Use a variety of activities to test the students. You could have several students doing different activities with the same structure/words. In this way you can tailor the test to the individual abilities.
- Encourage students to keep their own record of their tests at the back of their exercise books. Let them write a comment in L1 about their test; this is called SELF-ASSESSMENT. Ask them to look at their tests and to write, in L1, e.g.

> *I am pleased with my exercise on the names of the animals because I studied hard and I got them all right. I am not so pleased with exercise number (x) because I forgot to put the `-ing´ on the end of the words.*

Ask them to say which exercises they found difficult and which ones were easy, which exercises they liked and which ones they did not like.

This activity has two important uses. Firstly, it provides you with useful feedback about the students' assimilation of the work covered and, secondly, it asks the students to reflect on the work they have done. This will help you to integrate testing into the general classroom work.

- Discuss the results individually. While the class is doing a quiet exercise, walk around speaking to students one by one.
- If you are satisfied with the results of the class in general, reward them with a game or activity that you know the students like. You could give them the choice of three so that they know they have had the chance to choose.
- Assessment should be continuous. When you do the end of year reports, judge all the results and make an average.

"What about surprise tests?" It is questionable whether this kind of testing is suitable for assessment but if you do wish to use it, the following can be used as a guideline.

- Ask the students to work in groups or pairs so that the vulnerable students feel more protected.
- Award all members of the group the same mark.
- Reward a good mark with a game or activity that you know the students like. This reinforces the idea of teamwork.
- Only test elements that the students have worked with recently. Most young students have a short memory span. They may not remember vocabulary or structures from the previous term or even month unless they have been using them continuously. This is where the work of recycling becomes so important.
- Try dividing the class up into small groups. Call these *study groups*: it sounds terribly important! Tell the students that they have twenty minutes to study in their groups and then test the group. This method helps the students to acquire learning strategies and reinforces team work.

T A S K

Once you have your first set of tests, look at the results. Are they as good as you expected? Better? Worse? If some students have performed better than you expected, try increasing your demands slightly. Do not overdo it! If they are worse than you expected, look at the tasks you set. Are they too difficult? Were your instructions clear? If there is one or more activity which was clearly unsatisfactory, do it again in class as a group activity.

CHAPTER 15

Sociocultural themes

Sociocultural themes are now often introduced in subject areas at primary level, including English. Teachers sometimes find it hard to identify sociocultural themes unless these are expressly pointed out in the teacher's book. Here are some guidelines for identifying and using these in your English classes.

First, we should try to identify the different aspects of sociocultural education. These are, generally speaking, guidelines which we try to offer to the students for their daily interaction with other people and their environment. The following is a list of such areas:

… moral and social education
… tolerance and understanding of different ethnic groups
… caring for our environment
… understanding health and sexuality
… equality for boys and girls
… being a responsible consumer
… road safety.

You may well identify other areas of social or cultural education which you feel are particularly appropriate to the environment you are working in.

Identifying socio-cultural themes

In order to introduce this kind of cross-curricular education into our classes we need to look carefully at our course materials to identify appropriate themes in each coursebook unit. You might like to try the following approach.

Illustrations

Look carefully at the illustrations in your book. You will probably see many elements of society appearing in the pictures, e.g. illustrations of children from mixed ethnic groups, children with physical disabilities, children performing key activities such as using a zebra crossing and so on. Such illustrations provide the students with the opportunity to exercise judgement on what they observe, which is an important step in personal development.

Vocabulary

Look at the vocabulary objectives for the unit. They will usually be grouped into word families. Each can be used to illustrate a particular social theme, e.g.

… the parts of the body = understanding health and sexuality
… countries and nationalities = tolerance and understanding of different ethnic groups
… the street = road safety
… animals and nature = caring for the environment.

Songs and rhymes

Look at the words to your songs and rhymes. Some will reflect a social theme.

Stories

If you are using stories for your teaching, you may well find that the moral of the story reinforces a behavioural issue, like the importance of being honest.

Exploiting social issues in the classroom

Social issues can be introduced in the classroom either through the contents of your course materials or general interaction among the members of your class, e.g. moral and social education is clearly present in the way your students work in pairs and small groups. Equality for boys and girls is present in the distribution of tasks in the classroom, i.e. don't always ask the girls to do the clearing up!

Useful guidelines

- You will almost certainly find it necessary to speak to your students about social issues in L1 in order to provide them with some kind of framework. A five-minute question and answer session about the theme in L1 is acceptable, as this initial discussion serves as contextualisation for the theme. Once your students are aware of the context, change to your usual use of English.

- Social issues give the students the opportunity to express their opinions. Intervene if you feel that the conversation is getting silly.

- The older students in primary may try to provoke you by saying obviously controversial things, particularly with respect to health and sexuality. The trick is not to react! Look at them strangely as if they have said something very silly and ask the other students if they agree with this frivolous remark. If they persist, follow the usual channels for discipline.

- Ask the students to draw their own illustrations of social issues. Remember we are talking about conduct and behaviour; it is much easier for them to understand if it is seen through images rather than words. If your students like this activity you could extend it by asking them to create posters.

Most young children today are habitual consumers of media images displaying a wealth of examples of bad behaviour. Let the students use this knowledge to discuss and then illustrate their posters.

The different stages of development of your students will lead you naturally towards certain themes. Students at the end of the primary school stage should be made aware of the dangers of poor eating habits and stereotyped physical images. You can try the following activity as an exercise for reinforcing positive values.

- Ask the students in L1 to think about why they like their friends.

- Concentrate on adjectives which describe personality and ability rather than looks, and write the key words in English on the board.

- The students can then make a poster with a central description and small illustrations of each point.

I like my friend because she is:
HELPFUL She always helps me in class.
GOOD FUN She always laughs.
KIND She always listens to my problems.
HONEST She never says bad things about me.
My friend is a great basketball player and is fantastic at art.

For older primary children, you may wish to look at something more universal, e.g. tolerance towards different ethnic groups. Many children are familiar with images of ethnic violence from their television screens. You could use this knowledge.

- Chose a conflict which is relatively well known and show the students a map of the geographic area in question.

- Ask the students to make a 'Peace Poster' for the people in this area. This would reflect images that the students associate with peace and tolerance, such as children of different ethnic origin playing together.

- If there is a local campaign for sending aid to the area in question you could take advantage of this to make a class collection for people in need. This would involve:

  … finding out what was needed
  … making a list of what they could donate
  … bringing in the items and delivering them to the collection centre
  … making a diary in English of their co-operation.

Here is an example of a plan for a poster.

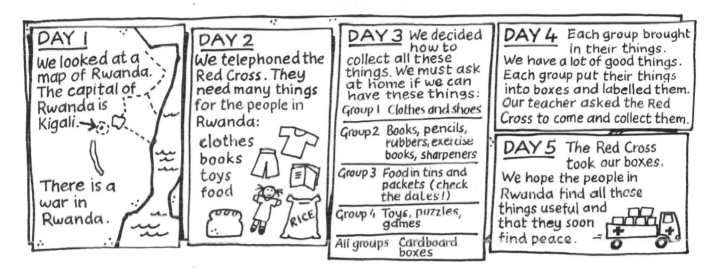

An activity of this nature should never be judgmental. You should avoid any mention of who is right and who is wrong. The students are simply participating in a co-operation campaign; they are not supporting a particular side.

It is often difficult to tailor the language needs of an English class to the input of social issues. Use your knowledge of the students' understanding of English to know how much English and how much L1 you should use; quite often you will find that a mixture is necessary.

Finally, use your knowledge of your students to guide you as to which social issues should be addressed. For example, if you are working with a class of girls and boys who are apparently not getting on very well, it would be advisable to reinforce the issue of equality. Or you could take advantage of the presence of different nationalities or ethnic groups in your class to talk about different countries and customs.

Look at the next unit in your coursebook and find a way of introducing a social theme. Work out how you can do this in class. When you have used it, reflect: how did it work? How did the students react? Will you do it differently next time? Are you satisfied with the English language content?

CHAPTER 16

Learning strategies

A new feature of many course materials is learning strategies: ways in which students comprehend, memorise and store new information.

Learning strategies are extremely personal and different for each student. There is not a right or wrong way of studying. However, study is a technique which must be taught and learned; it is not instinctive. For this reason we try to provide the students with various models to choose from. Once the students have been presented with several different options they must choose for themselves which strategy they feel will best suit their learning style. It is important to point out to the students that they must learn for themselves; you cannot learn for them.

Comprehension

Learning strategies for structural language will usually involve the students doing some sort of activity which displays comprehension of the grammar rules involved. They may be asked to make rules for a particular structure or to underline the correct explanation of the rule, e.g.

> Look at the sentences.
>
> 1 I lived in Africa when I was young.
>
> 2 Maria didn't live in my street.
>
> 3 Did your mother live near her school?
>
> 4 Picasso lived in France.
>
> Now make a rule: When do we put *d* on *live*?

The idea of this kind of exercise is that the students must understand the mechanism of the auxiliary verb. This does not mean that they will never make a mistake with it once they understand, but it does make it easier when you have to correct them. The complexity of these activities will, obviously, depend on the age of your class. The younger the children are, the simpler the activity will be, e.g.

> Look at this paragraph.
>
> Bobby and Sally live in Manchester. They go to school by bus. On Saturdays they play football for a local club. This year Sally is the captain of their team, the Manchester Juniors.
>
> Now make a rule: When do we use capital letters?

Memorising

These strategies are used mainly for vocabulary and can easily be performed as games and puzzles which make them much more fun for the classroom. FLASHCARDS are a useful resource for memory games

Probably the best method of stimulating memory for vocabulary is by making sure that the children see and hear the words as much as possible. Learning long lists of irregular verbs or vocabulary results in them learning the words parrot fashion, but being totally unable to use the words they have learned.

Here are some ideas for helping children to learn vocabulary.

- Ask yourself how useful the word is going to be to the students. Remember that students will only remember words that they use. Do they really need to know the names of ten different types of bird? If you are teaching in a rural environment it may well be useful for them to know some different types of bird, but ten is excessive. Limit the number to the most useful.

- Consider whether the vocabulary you are teaching falls within a normal field of interest for your students. For example, the names of different types of materials (*plastic, leather, cotton, nylon*) are of little interest to a primary class. However if you situate this vocabulary within a field of interest for them it will be much easier for them to learn, e.g. *Think of all the different materials we use for a football match. What is the ball made of? It can be leather or plastic. What is the difference? Which is best? What is your football strip made of? It can be nylon or cotton. Which do you prefer?*

- Limit the amount of vocabulary that you expect your students to learn at a time. Three to five words for the younger students and five to ten words for the older ones is more than enough.

- Ask them to learn their vocabulary in two stages. The first stage is to learn how to use the words, e.g. ask the students to learn five words about the house: *bedroom, bathroom, kitchen, sitting room, garage.* Then test them orally first by asking them to give examples of what you do in each different room, e.g. *Where do you sleep?* (In the bedroom.) *Where do you put the car?* (In the garage.).

  The second stage involves learning how to write the words. Rather than asking them to write out a list, give the students a picture of a house and ask them to label the rooms.

  In this way the students will learn their vocabulary over two or three sessions. This will give you the opportunity to monitor the students to see who is learning and who is not. If the students are having difficulty with, e.g. stage two, which involves learning how to write the words, you can use simpler methods to start them off. Try using some of the word games described in Chapter 7.

Remember to keep recycling vocabulary from previous units. Primary school students cannot be expected to work on the vocabulary in their coursebooks on their own initiative. Recycling is a building activity. As you test your students on their new vocabulary, make sure that you always include something from the previous units. Let's take the example of the five words about the house again. You could recycle them in the following ways.

- If you are studying prepositions: *The bedroom is next to the bathroom. The kitchen is between the sitting room and the garage.*

- If you are studying comparatives: *The bedroom is bigger than the bathroom.*

- If you are studying *There is/are*: *There is a chair in the sitting room. There are two tables in the kitchen.*

Furthermore, brightly coloured posters, projects, labelling of the classroom and other visual aids will help your students to use the vocabulary they have learned.

◆ SEE CHAPTER 10

Storing vocabulary

Your students will inevitably forget some of the vocabulary they have learned. You need to teach them a practical way of storing their vocabulary so that they can refer to it in the future.

There are a variety of methods for storing vocabulary; your choice of method will depend largely on the age and ability of your students. However, it is advisable to offer the students a variety of storage systems in order to take into account different learning strategies and to avoid making the task too routine.

The following is a suggestion of three possible stages for vocabulary storing, starting with a simple system for the younger students and leading to a more sophisticated method for encouraging the students to improve and expand their vocabulary.

Flashcards

This is an ideal method for young children who are still coming to terms with reading and writing in their own language. You can vary the FLASHCARDS as you progress through the school year. Try the Letter Box activity on PAGE 60 as a method of storing vocabulary.

If your students have their own FLASHCARDS, they might need to glue an envelope on the inside cover of their coursebook for storing them. Be prepared for your students to lose their FLASHCARDS or for accidents when they are cutting out and colouring in. They can always make a substitute. ◆ SEE CHAPTER 10

Word families

PHOTOCOPIABLE PAGE 6 gives ideas for making large posters with the vocabulary as you finish each unit. The poster can then be hung up as a constant reminder. You can exploit this throughout the year by setting up vocabulary competitions.

- Divide the class into teams.
- Stand Team A with their backs to one of the posters but let the other teams see the poster.
- Team A has to say all the words that are in the container.
- Give them one point for each word.
- When they cannot remember a word, the other teams have to mime or describe the word.
- When Team A guesses the word, give half a point to Team A and half a point to the team which mimed or described the word.

Alternatively, you can do spot checks by taking down a poster or making the students sit with their backs to it and asking the students to write all the words down. They can work individually or in pairs. The students who finish first shout *STOP!*

Wall dictionary

We have mentioned several times that the best way to encourage your students to memorise their vocabulary is by offering them visual stimuli. An interesting way to do this to make a wall dictionary. This is a permanent frieze which you build on over the year.

- Choose an image that is appropriate to the age of your students and that visualises the idea of vocabulary belonging in a particular place. As an example we shall use a train. This is for younger students. If you are teaching older students, you might prefer a ladder or a shelf.

- Draw the outline of a steam train on a long sheet of white paper. Draw a wagon for each of the different word families that you will be using over the year, e.g. the family, the house, animals, food, etc. Make sure that each wagon is big enough to hold all the words you want your students to know.
- Paint each wagon a different colour and paint in some background: trees, sky, a river, a bridge, etc. The students will enjoy helping you.
- As you finish working with one word family, usually at the end of a coursebook unit, make small cards of the words and glue them on one of the wagons.
- Work progressively, building up the train wagon after wagon.
- Use the wall dictionary to play one of the games in *Word families* above.
- As the train gets more and more loaded, you can play with the imagery. Tell the students, in L1: *With so many people on the train it is easy for somebody to get left behind at the station! Let's just check that everyone is on board.* Play one of the memory games described above to check that they remember all the vocabulary covered so far.

Storing structures

Storing structures is much more difficult than storing vocabulary. You will probably find it easier if you look at this area as 'whole language' rather than just structures. Structures on their own mean very little to the students and it is unlikely that they will learn them just by writing out lists of grammar rules.

The need to store structures comes as the students build up their structural base to the language. Younger students, who are perhaps only working with the verbs *to be* and *have got* in the present tense over the course of a year, will probably not need to store these verb structures as they will be using them continuously.

The problem arises when the students are working with several different verb tenses and need to be reminded of how each one works. The different structures will each lend themselves to a particular kind of visual display.

Let's look at one example of how to display a verb tense. By putting tenses into context, you will make it easier for the students to remember them. Students can make these displays in the form of a poster or in their exercise books.

In the past

- Make up a questionnaire in class for the students to take home and do with their parents or grandparents.
- Students can then work in small groups to make posters (as on the following page) about life in the past. They can glue a copy of the questionnaire to the centre of the poster and draw pictures to illustrate the answers. Under each picture they can write one of the answers from their group selection, e.g. *Miguel's grandmother didn't go to school.*
  Paula's mother did all the cooking, because she didn't have a mother.

1 Miguel's grandmother didn't go to school.

2 Ana's father left school when he was 14 years old.

3 Roberto's mother only had one doll.

1 When did you first go to school?

2 When did you leave school?

3 What toys did you have?

4 Did your mother work outside the house?

5 Did your father have a car?

6 Did you have a television/computer/video/bicycle?

7 What did you do to help at home?

7 Paula's mother did all the cooking because she didn't have a mother.

6 Pablo's grandfather had a bicycle but he didn't have a computer.

4 Raul's grandmother worked in a factory.

5 Elisa's father had the first car in his village.

Word maps

Once you begin dealing with more complex word areas you can try getting the students to store their words using 'maps', e.g.

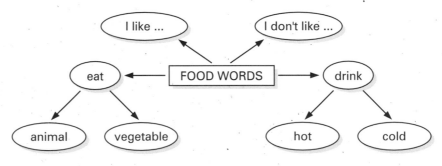

Word maps can be as simple or as complex as you wish to make them. If you feel, for example, that the map above would be too complex for your students, you could ask them to classify their food words into the different meals of the day, e.g.

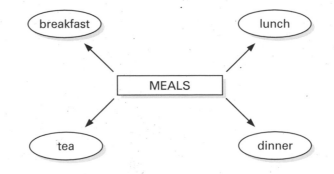

If you are using word maps, it is a good idea to include an element of personalised classification, for example the *I like/I don't like* boxes. This will provide you with an exploitation activity comparing the students' diagrams. *How many students like salad? Who doesn't like milk?*

Student responsibility

We have looked at some of the ways that you can teach your students to learn but it is important that they understand that learning is their responsibility. When you start teaching the younger primary school students, you may find that they are totally dependent on you for everything. Part of your more general task is to teach your students to be independent. This is a gradual process which you can build on in the following way.

- The first stage of autonomy is to teach children to be responsible for their class materials. Find a place for the students to leave their books and pencil cases. The only books they might need to take home are their activity books and exercise books. The rest should be left at school in their locker or desk. This will minimise the number of times that students forget their books.

- Children must be taught to look after all the things that they use in the classroom, especially the things that are not theirs. You can start this by teaching them to look after their own things. Encourage them to make their books look attractive by illustrating and colouring in their activities; this also makes their work personal. Do not let them scribble all over their coursebooks and activity books. If they do this, they will also be likely to scribble on any books you have as class sets, such as guided readers.

- Set aside some time at the end of the class for tidying up the classroom, especially after a messy activity like painting. Make your classroom as attractive as possible with work that the children have produced. If you do not have your own English classroom, see if you can negotiate a space on the wall for your work. Change the wall displays as you produce new work.

- Once your students are learning to be responsible for their belongings and their classroom, you can start to demand responsibility in their learning.

- Study groups are a good way of introducing responsibility for learning (SEE PAGE 74). Students will find it easier if their responsibility is collective. They will also help each other to learn.

- With older students you can demand personal responsibility for their study. Start gradually, asking them to study a few words (not more than ten at a time) for a quick test. Do not expect them to do anything alone that has not been dealt with thoroughly in class. Ask them to study new vocabulary after you have finished the practice stage in class and not before.

- Homework is a question of personal opinion among teachers. Primary teachers often decide not to give homework, for the reason that children get tired enough spending hours at school, without doing further work in the evening. If you (or your school) feel that homework is necessary, ensure you vary it (i.e. not all writing exercises – do some memorisation, some reading, etc.) and that you use it to feed into the classroom work, e.g. researching for projects, asking the family questions.

Design a different structure poster for a something that you are working with, e.g. prepositions or adjectives. Can you think of other ways of displaying structures, something that gets the students doing things with the structure?

Moving on

Independently of the suggestions in this book, it is important to be prepared to draw on personal resources as well as on our professional knowledge.

Course materials are not the only devices that we have for teaching. As teachers we are the central resource for the classroom and for our students. It is essential to be flexible in our use of ready-prepared materials and to make them work for us and for our students.

By understanding some of the mechanisms involved in designing the working materials for a primary school classroom, we are better placed to design our own materials to supplement and support the coursebook. (For more on this, see DEVELOPING RESOURCES FOR PRIMARY in the same series.)

From a purely theoretical point of view, we tend to look at the ideal situation: excellent training facilities for teachers, in-service training on a regular basis, small groups of quiet, bright, highly motivated students, stimulating home environments, perfect teaching facilities, unlimited supplies of resources for the classroom and other such fantasies! In practice, more often than not, we are working in a less than ideal environment and have to adapt our materials and teaching programmes to suit each class.

We have looked at some of the problems that may arise in the classroom and discussed some ways of dealing with them. However, by far the best way to solve problems is to avoid them in the first place. Many conflicts in the classroom can be avoided by using the GROUP DYNAMICS we have looked at. Unsuccessful results can be avoided by tailoring our expectations to the real situation in the classroom and disruptive behaviour can often be avoided by keeping the students busy with imaginative and active tasks.

It is by developing our own skills that we are able to transform our classroom into a lively learning environment. Teacher development is an ongoing task. We all need to take time to sit back and question what we are doing in the classroom, adapt and change our activities. In this way we can achieve dynamic and active learning, which is stimulating for both us and our students.

1 Checklist to evaluate course materials

Title of book: ....

1 Number of students in class: ....

   This book is for: large groups ☐   small groups ☐   both ☐

2 This book is aimed at .... age range

   According to school records the class standard is: appropriate for age ☐

                                                  lower than actual age ☐

                                                  higher than actual age ☐

3 Balance of skills in sample unit

   Number of exercises: listening .... speaking .... reading .... writing ....

4 Date of publication: ....

5 Number of teaching hours in school year: ....

   Number of estimated teaching hours in book: ....

   Number of estimated hours for extra activities: ....

   Total number of hours: ....

6 Proportion of text to illustration

   Coursebook:

   no text ☐   25% text ☐   50% text ☐   75% text ☐   no illustrations ☐

   Activity book:

   no text ☐   25% text ☐   50% text ☐   75% text ☐   no illustrations ☐

7 Components

   Core:

   Coursebook ☐   Activity Book ☐   Cassette ☐   Teacher's Book ☐

   Supplementary:

   Flashcards ☐   Posters ☐   Student's Cassettes ☐   Evaluation Pack ☐

   Picture Dictionary ☐   Video ☐   Cut-out Book ☐

8 Are the themes of the units appropriate for your students? yes ☐   no ☐

9 Recycling units: yes ☐   no ☐   If yes, how often? ....

10 Total price of all necessary components:

   For the student: ....

   For the school: ....

An Introduction to Teaching English to Children, © Susan House, 1997

SEE PAGE 20

THE SWEET SHOP

Listen and circle.

1 There are TWO/THREE/FOUR people in the shop.

2 Bobby and Liz are buying SWEETS/ICE-CREAMS.

3 Mrs Jackson is a SHOPKEEPER/POLICEWOMAN/DOCTOR.

Now draw your own party bag with lots of different sweets.

Listen and write.

1 The party bags are for S_ _'_ party.

2 Party bags have d_ _ _ _ _ _ _ _ sweets in them.

3 The children want t_ _ _ _ _ party bags.

4 E_ _ _ _ _ people are coming to the party.

An Introduction to Teaching English to Children, © Susan House, 1997 **PHOTOCOPIABLE**

RULES FOR OUR CLASSROOM

DO

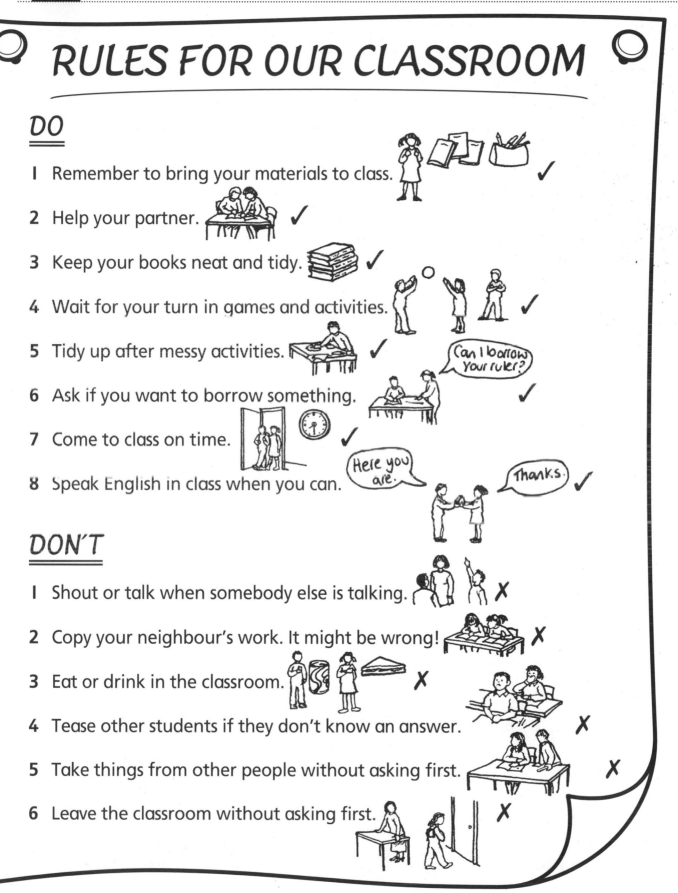

1 Remember to bring your materials to class.

2 Help your partner.

3 Keep your books neat and tidy.

4 Wait for your turn in games and activities.

5 Tidy up after messy activities.

6 Ask if you want to borrow something.

7 Come to class on time.

8 Speak English in class when you can.

DON'T

1 Shout or talk when somebody else is talking.

2 Copy your neighbour's work. It might be wrong!

3 Eat or drink in the classroom.

4 Tease other students if they don't know an answer.

5 Take things from other people without asking first.

6 Leave the classroom without asking first.

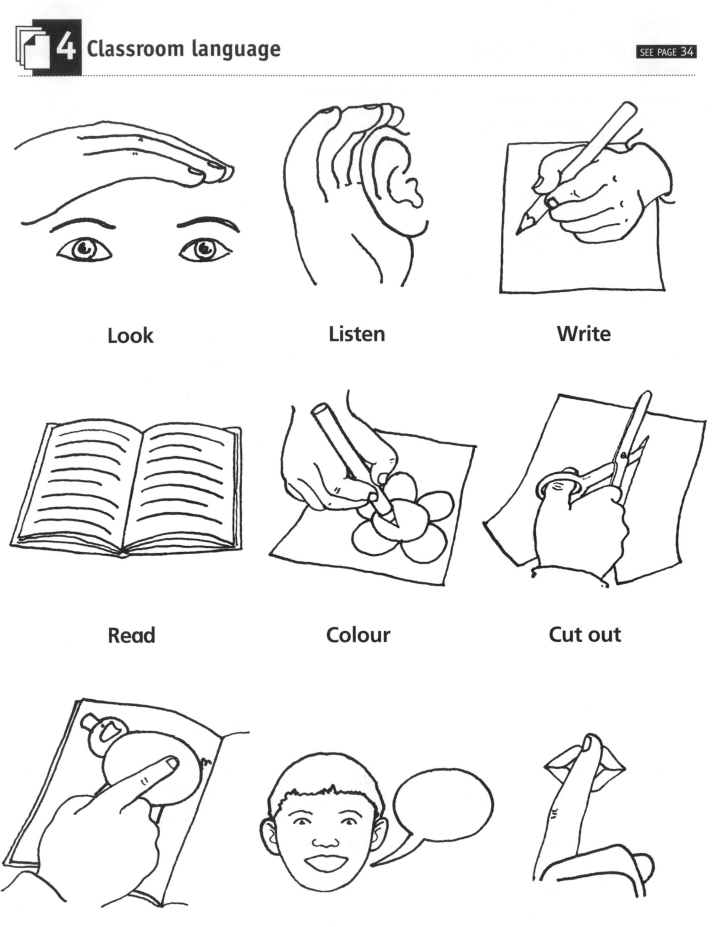

Look

Listen

Write

Read

Colour

Cut out

Show me

Tell me

Be quiet

An Introduction to Teaching English to Children, © Susan House, 1997 **PHOTOCOPIABLE**

two	hot
blue	dog
shoe	song
you	lot
new	got
do	copy
who	doll
to	lorry
look	book
don't	some

SEE PAGE 43

An Introduction to Teaching English to Children, © Susan House, 1997 **PHOTOCOPIABLE**

7 Framework for lesson planning
SEE PAGE 52

LESSON PLAN

Aim: ....
Key vocabulary: .... Key structure: ....
Pronunciation: ....
Socio-cultural activity: ....
Recycling: ....
Materials: ....

STARTING THE CLASS

....
....

Time: ....

PRESENTATION
Step 1: ....

Time: ....

Step 2: ....

Time: ....

PRACTICE
Step 1: ....

Time: ....

Step 2: ....

Time: ....

RECYCLING
Step 1: ....
....
....

Step 2: ....
....

Time: ....

FINISHING THE CLASS

....

Time: ....

TOTAL TIME = ...

SEE PAGE 64

An Introduction to Teaching English to Children, © Susan House, 1997 **PHOTOCOPIABLE**

9 Student assessment record SEE PAGE 71

STUDENT ASSESSMENT RECORD

NAME: .... CLASS: ....

AGE: .... AVERAGE AGE IN CLASS: ....

DATE OF ASSESSMENT: .... ABSENT THIS TERM: ....

1 Continuous assessment of classwork

Excellent progress ☐   Satisfactory progress ☐   Unsatisfactory progress ☐

2 General attitude and effort

Participation in class: Excellent ☐ Satisfactory ☐ Unsatisfactory ☐

Presentation of work: Excellent ☐ Satisfactory ☐ Unsatisfactory ☐

Co-operation with peers: Excellent ☐ Satisfactory ☐ Unsatisfactory ☐

Completion of tasks: Excellent ☐ Satisfactory ☐ Unsatisfactory ☐

Average mark for attitude and effort: Excellent ☐ Satisfactory ☐ Unsatisfactory ☐

Overall comment for 1 and 2:   Excellent ☐ Satisfactory ☐ Unsatisfactory ☐

3 Oral tests

Marks out of ten:

Test 1 ☐ 2 ☐ 3 ☐ 4 ☐ 5 ☐ 6 ☐

Average mark out of ten: ....

4 Written tests

Marks out of ten:

Test 1 ☐ 2 ☐ 3 ☐ 4 ☐ 5 ☐ 6 ☐

Average mark out of ten: ....

Average mark for 3 and 4: ....

Observations: ....

....

An Introduction to Teaching English to Children, © Susan House, 1997

Glossary

ACCURACY

When students are accurate, they do not make any mistakes. Accuracy work concentrates on practising language in order to perfect a particular structure, sound, etc. (Compare FLUENCY.)

ACQUISITION

Compare this with 'learning'. If students learn something, they make a conscious effort to master it, as with a second language. Children acquire their own language through experience - they are 'surrounded' by it. It is important to try to create situations which will help students 'acquire' the second language.

CONTINUOUS ASSESSMENT

The system of testing and evaluating a group of students on a regular basis in order to build up a picture of their abilities and progress.

FLASHCARDS

Large cards with pictures and/or words on for use in the classroom, either by the teacher, e.g. in drills, or by the students, e.g. in games.

FLUENCY

When students can talk or write without a lot of hesitation, they are said to be fluent. They are not necessarily accurate. Fluency work concentrates on getting a message across, i.e. communicating effectively, not on perfect language. (Compare ACCURACY.)

GROUP DYNAMICS

This refers to the way you organise your class, e.g. groups, pairwork, etc. and the way in which they interact.

LEARNING STRATEGIES

How students learn. It is now accepted that the teacher cannot do everything for the students – they have to accept responsiblity for their own learning and each person has to develop their own ways of learning.

PERSONALISATION

Making a situation/structure fit a student's own life so that they can talk or write about themselves, e.g. applying *have got* to children's toys, pets, clothes, etc.

PRODUCTIVE

Language which students are expected to understand and produce (through speaking or writing) in different contexts. (Compare RECEPTIVE.)

REALIA

Materials from the 'real world' brought into the classroom for practice, e.g. using a TV guide to choose/discuss programmes.

RECEPTIVE

Language which students will understand when they read or listen. They are not expected to produce it. (Compare PRODUCTIVE.)

ROLEPLAY

Any activity which entails students taking on different roles, i.e. they pretend to be someone else, such as a shop assistant and a customer.

SELF-ASSESSMENT

Students look at their own work and decide for themselves if they are pleased with it or not. They therefore judge themselves.

TOTAL PHYSICAL RESPONSE (TPR)

Students respond physically to an instruction, e.g. they stand up, hold up a FLASHCARD, etc. It is thought that children learn more easily if they are able to react to language in a physical way.

Further reading

Teacher's Guides

Cant, A and Superfine, W *Developing Resources for Primary* Richmond Publishing, 1997
A collection of resources, activities, games, etc. for the primary English classroom, all presented in such a way that teachers can transfer the ideas to other topics of language in the classroom.

Halliwell, S *Teaching English in the Primary Classroom* Addison Wesley Longman, 1992 (5th edition)
This helps teachers who are at the stage of introducing English into the primary classroom and provides useful ideas for cross-curricular work.

Phillips, S *Young Learners* OUP, 1993
This is useful for teachers who have little experience of working with young children. It is useful for deciding objectives for this age group.

Scott, W and Ytreberg, L *Teaching English to Children* Addison Wesley Longman, 1990
Useful ideas for activities concentrating on skills-based teaching.

Wright, A *Storytelling with Children* OUP, 1996
A useful resource with many practical ideas for using traditional stories and creating stories with children.

Resources

Bourke, K *The Jungle Grammar Books* OUP, 1996

Byrne, D *Roundabout Wall Pictures* Phoenix ELT

Palim, J and Power, P *Jamboree* Addison Wesley Longman, 1990
Activities for oral work with young children, and a clear guide for the teacher.

Retter, C and Valls, N *Bonanza* Addison Wesley Longman, 1993 (7th edition)
This book provides games for the classroom and flashcards to cut out.

Toth, M *Heinemann Children's Games* Heinemann, 1994

Hotshot Puzzles OUP

Materials for Language Teaching Series Phoenix ELT

Polka Dot Playlets Addison Wesley Longman
A series of six stories which can then be performed as plays, with plenty of teacher support.

Song books (*Count me in, Sing-a-story, Game-songs with Prof Dogg's Troupe*) A & C Black

Readers

A Scary Story Night Collection Phoenix ELT

Heinemann Children's Readers Heinemann

Longman Young Readers: Stripey Short Stories Addison Wesley Longman

Oxford Storyland Readers OUP

Spellbinders OUP

Index of topics

Index of activities and language

(the numbers in brackets refer to photocopiable pages)